POWERFUL PALEO SUPERFOODS

First published in the USA in 2014 by
Fair Winds Press, a member of
Quarto Publishing Group USA Inc.
100 Cummings Center
Suite 406-L
Beverly, MA 01915-6101
www.fairwindspress.com
Visit www.QuarrySPOON.com and help us celebrate food and
culture one spoonful at a time!

18 17 16 15 14   2 3 4 5

ISBN: 978-1-59233-597-8

Digital edition published in 2014
eISBN: 978-1-62788-015-2

Library of Congress Cataloging-in-Publication Data available

Cover design by Duckie Designs
Book design by Duckie Designs
Book layout by meganjonesdesign.com
Photography by Heather Connell
Images courtesy of Shutterstock.com: pages 28, 31, 34, 38, 42, 46,
50, 62, 66, 74, 77, 80, 86, 90, 94, 98, 102, 108, 116, 124, 132, 136, 158,
166, 170, 173, 176, 180, 186, 190, 198, 202, 206, 210

Printed and bound in China

The information in this book is for educational purposes only. It is
not intended to replace the advice of a physician or medical prac-
titioner. Please see your health care provider before beginning
any new health program.

POWERFUL
PALEO
SUPERFOODS

THE BEST PRIMAL-FRIENDLY FOODS FOR BURNING FAT, BUILDING MUSCLE AND OPTIMAL HEALTH

HEATHER CONNELL, R.H.N.C.
AUTHOR OF *PALEO SWEETS & TREATS*
WITH JULIA MARANAN

To Scott, Clair, and Laine, who are the loves of
my life and bring so much happiness to my day.
—Heather

To Dan and Joshua, who make every day
better than I could have asked for or imagined.
—Julia

CONTENTS

CHAPTER 4: PALEO SUPER FRUITS | 111

CHAPTER 5: PALEO SUPER FATS | 153

CHAPTER 6: PALEO SUPER HERBS AND SPICES | 185

INTRODUCTION

THE BASICS OF EATING PALEO

My Paleo life started in 2011. I had been suffering for several months with health issues, which led to doctor visit after doctor visit with no answers. I was frustrated. I was tired. I was mad—and I needed to make changes. But what did I need to change, and where did I need to start? I started with my diet, and it's there where I found the culprits—gluten, dairy, and soy. Within forty days of switching my diet to a Paleo lifestyle, the health issues that had been a constant presence simply disappeared.

In my journey living a Paleo lifestyle these past few years, I have not only transformed my health, but I have also come to appreciate and love REAL FOOD. At its heart, Paleo is about eating foods that are REAL, or as I like to explain to my kids, the superheroes of the food world. I believe that if you can find food grown in naturally nutrient-rich soil (or meat from animals fed their natural diets), you are pretty much guaranteed to have the right balance of vitamins and minerals to not just survive, but thrive. After studying nutritional science, I understand why certain foods that are often overlooked or rejected by health experts, such as coconut oil and grass-fed beef, actually qualify as superfoods in the Paleo community, and why they deserve a place at your table. Now it's my turn to share with you the "whys." It's my hope that this book will help you incorporate Paleo super-foods into your diet so you can feel your best, too.

WHAT IS "PALEO"?

The Paleo (or, Paleolithic) diet is a lifestyle based on the ancestral human diet. The Paleo diet (or lifestyle) has been called many things: Caveman Diet, Primal Diet, Real Food Diet, even MVF, which stands for Meat-Vegetables-Fat. All these terms refer to basically the same way of eating—the eating habits of our hunter-gatherer Paleolithic ancestors who, if they were able to avoid illness (due to the lack of modern medicine), lived very long and healthy lives.

Although we can't know exactly what our hunter-gatherer ancestors ate, in principle, Paleo is about eating the same whole foods that were found in nature millions of years ago. These include foods that come from the land, such as meats, vegetables, fruits, nuts, and seeds, and foods that come from open waters, such as fish and shellfish. These foods are nutrient-dense and are free from all those modern ingredients you can't pronounce. When we remove inflammatory foods from our diet—foods that were not part of our ancestors' daily meals, such as wheat flour, industrial seed oils, sugar, and even supposedly healthy foods such as grains, dairy, and soy—we reduce the risk of the most prevalent diseases of our civilization: heart disease, cancer, obesity, autoimmune diseases, and diabetes. Additionally (and best of all), we feel better, our energy levels rise, we look years younger, and we sleep better.

WHAT CAN YOU EAT ON THE PALEO DIET?

HERE IS THE "YES" LIST, OR WHAT I LIKE TO CALL THE "REAL" FOOD LIST

First, eat whole foods! Beyond that, the idea is to rely on foods that our hunter-gatherer forbears ate because our bodies are particularly well designed to digest them and to use the nutrients they offer. Here is a short rundown of those foods and why they make the Paleo YES list. The rest of the book focuses on Paleo superfoods within each category that are your absolute best choices.

MEATS AND EGGS: Although conventional dietary advice recommends limiting animal products, a look into their nutritional profiles will quickly show you that these foods are incredibly concentrated sources of many nutrients, including vitamin B_{12}, zinc, and iron. They also provide complete protein, which means they contain all of the amino acids required by the body. Not that all animal foods are created equal—read on to find out which ones earn the title of superfood (and why your meats and eggs should always come from grass- and organic-fed, pastured-raised, and sustainable sources).

SEAFOOD AND SHELLFISH: These foods are excellent sources of protein and rich omega-3 fatty acids, plus vitamins and minerals. As such, they're an important component of a balanced Paleo diet that includes high-quality animal products. Seafood consumption has been linked to a reduced risk of many diseases, which we will talk about more specifically in the chapters ahead. Wild-caught seafood and shellfish are your best bet.

VEGETABLES: A slew of scientific studies have shown the incredible benefits of the health-promoting nutrients in vegetables. While many other diets prominently feature vegetables, there are several that are particularly important to the Paleo lifestyle. Those superfoods are the ones we'll focus on here. There is an abundance of vegetables from season to season, which gives you no excuse not to include one (or two) on your plate all year-round. Frozen organic vegetables are also an option since they are usually flash frozen right after harvesting, preserving their nutrients. Make sure the variety you choose doesn't have any other additives, such as salt.

FRUITS: These flavorful, refreshing gems are full of healthful nutrients. Modern fruits may be larger and sweeter—thus, containing more fructose—than in centuries past, so I recommend eating lower-sugar fruits like many of the ones listed in this book. Choose in-season and locally grown fruits for the best taste and the most nutrients. Frozen organic fruits are fine as well, just read the label to make sure there are no added sugars.

NUTS AND SEEDS: They may be small in size, but they are big when it comes to nutrition. Nuts and seeds are not only a rich source of vitamins and minerals, but many of them also contain monounsaturated fats and phytonutrients (healthful substances found in plant foods) that do wonders for promoting overall health. However, just because nuts and seeds were available to our ancestors doesn't mean you should consume vast quantities of them, or that all nuts and seeds are equally good for you. Many kinds contain "anti-nutrients," such as phytic acid and lectin—which bind to iron, zinc, and calcium, among other minerals, so your body can't use them—and nuts and seeds are frequently high in omega-6s, which most people already consume too much of. I'll tell you which nuts and seeds qualify as Paleo superfoods and which you should limit.

HEALTHY FATS: Many nutrition experts now recognize that mono- and polyunsaturated fats in foods such as avocado, coconut, and olive oil help your body absorb crucial vitamins, minerals, and phytochemicals from the other foods you eat. But the Paleo diet also includes high-quality animal fats—especially omega-3 essential fatty acids—that help your body function optimally. The chapters ahead discuss which healthy fats you should focus on.

THE "NO" LIST

The primary Paleo principle here is to get rid of the junk! That means all processed and packaged foods, of course, but also some foods that are seemingly healthy. If you need more convincing to remove these foods from your diet, maybe these reasons will do the trick. (See the Resources section, page 214, for a list of my favorite websites, blogs, and books to learn more about the nutritional science behind the Paleo diet and why these foods might actually be harming your health.)

PROCESSED AND PACKAGED FOODS: This category includes anything you pick up in a drive-thru window, anything housed in a colorful cardboard or plastic box, anything with a long list of ingredients you don't recognize or can't pronounce, and almost anything you can find in the middle aisles of your grocery store. Basically, anything that is not real food. These foods are less nutritious and more calorie-dense then their fresh, natural counterparts. In fact, these foods act like "negative nutrition," meaning they take more from your body than they give. Most processed foods are concentrated carbohydrates, so consuming them leads to rapid rises in blood sugar and large amounts of insulin flooding your body. Over time, this increases your risk of obesity, diabetes, and heart disease, among other health problems. Processed foods also generally have large amounts of added sodium (bad for blood pressure) and added chemical substitutes for fat (so they can be called "low-fat" or "fat-free") to appeal to your taste buds.

ADDED SUGARS: Added sugars—including granulated sugar, brown sugar, artificial sugars, and agave nectar—all trigger spikes in blood sugar and require your body to secrete large amounts of insulin to keep your blood sugar in a healthy range. These high levels of blood sugar and insulin are inflammatory in the body and promote disorders such as insulin resistance, diabetes, and obesity. These processed, concentrated sugars also do not contain any vitamins, minerals, or phytochemicals that contribute to your overall health; all they do add is empty calories. They're also in an astonishing number of packaged and prepared foods, even those that don't taste especially sweet, like ketchup and salad dressings.

GRAINS AND GRAIN-LIKE SEEDS: These include, but are not limited to, wheat, barley, rye, spelt, corn, rice, quinoa, millet, bulgur wheat, buckwheat, and amaranth (and foods made with these). The prevailing nutritional opinion says that whole grains should make up a significant part of your diet, but Paleo proponents recognize that they may do more harm than good to our bodies. Carbohydrate-dense grains promote elevated insulin levels that can lead to heart disease and diabetes. They tend to be high in omega-6s, exacerbating the imbalance of omega-6s and omega-3s that most of us have and that contributes to a whole host of modern diseases. Grains also contain lectins, plant proteins that prevent you from absorbing certain nutrients (such as calcium) and can cause damage to your intestinal lining, which then leads to an imbalance of gut bacteria and provokes systemic inflammation. Inflammation can cause health problems such as asthma, allergies, migraines, joint pain, skin conditions, fertility issues, and other things you might never think to associate with what you eat.

LEGUMES: Legumes (and grains, for that matter) weren't typically part of the human diet until the agricultural revolution. And although today they're a mainstay of vegetarian and vegan diets, legumes unfortunately aren't exactly the health food they're made out to be. Although they do contain protein, vitamins, and minerals, their protein is incomplete (unlike animal products, they don't contain all of the amino acids we need), and because of their high carbohydrate concentration, they don't count as nutrient-dense. In addition, all beans (including, but not limited to, black, pinto, kidney, white, and garbanzo), lentils, peas, and peanuts contain inflammatory lectins plus other anti-nutrients such as phytates that can rob the body of valuable minerals.

SOY: Soy is, in fact, a legume, but I pulled it out from the previous discussion because it hides in so many of our processed foods (read your labels!) and has some unique characteristics. For instance, soy contains high concentrations of phytoestrogens, plant-based compounds that mimic estrogen in our bodies. There's a lot of conflicting research about whether soy's phytoestrogens increase the risk of hormone-dependent cancers such as breast cancer, but given soy's other drawbacks, the decision to avoid soy seems like a clear one. In addition to containing anti-nutrients such as phytic acid—which binds to iron, zinc, and calcium, among other minerals, so your body can't use them— soy contains substances called trypsin inhibitors that make it difficult to digest proteins properly.

DAIRY: This includes cow, sheep, and goat milk or cheese, and anything made with these. Milk is one of the eight most common food allergens, and the milk proteins casein and whey are usually to blame. People with type 1 diabetes and celiac disease produce higher than normal levels of antibodies in response to casein, suggesting that dairy can aggravate these and potentially other autoimmune conditions, notes a study in *Hormone and Metabolic Research*. And though you've probably been told to down dairy to help strengthen your bones, many studies on fracture risk don't find that milk benefits bone health at all, and there's increasing evidence that consuming too much dairy might increase the risk of ovarian and prostate cancer. Several of the Paleo superfoods in this book are much better choices for boosting bone health. Read on to find out what you *should* be eating!

WHAT ARE THE SUPERFOODS OF THE PALEO WORLD?

Superfoods are a special class of foods that are nutritionally dense, meaning they provide a high number of health-promoting nutrients for the calories they contain. It's important to eat a variety of nutrient-rich foods, such as the fifty Paleo superfoods in this book, because nutrients don't work in isolation but synergistically. The powerful interaction between these vitamins, minerals, fats, antioxidants, and other substances plays a major role in your overall health and longevity, and in keeping your body and mind functioning at their peak.

This book guides you through fifty foods that you can rely on as the foundation of your Paleo lifestyle. The superfoods listed here are all REAL foods (not food products) that provide plenty of health benefits and that can have a profound impact on the way you feel. They are among the best foods to provide you with 100 percent of all the nutrients you need every day, and you will soon see that they are also some of the most flavorful foods you will ever place on your plate. The delicious and totally doable recipes in this book will help you incorporate these foods into your diet, whether you're looking for a fresh way to prepare an old favorite or just want to try an unfamiliar food.

QUALIFICATIONS TO BE A PALEO SUPERFOOD

For a food to be included on the list of Paleo superfoods, it needs to meet strict criteria for nutrition—rich in nutrients such as vitamins, minerals, fiber, protein, essential fatty acids, and antioxidants. Additionally, it needs to promote health and vitality in the body. And most important, all the health claims of these foods have to be supported by scientific literature. Because each food offers a unique nutritional profile that contributes to your optimal health, it is also important that this list contain enough variety to fulfill your nutritional needs, while deliciously appealing to your taste buds. But you could pick up any superfoods book and find foods that meet these qualifications. Why do these fifty foods deserve a spot on your Paleo plate?

THEY ARE ANTI-INFLAMMATORY.

The typical modern diet includes lots of highly processed foods, inflammation-promoting fats, simple carbohydrates, and other substances that trigger the chronic inflammation responsible for some of the biggest health ills we face today, including cardiovascular disease, diabetes, and cancer. Thanks to their anti-inflammatory omega-3 fatty acids and phytochemicals, many of these Paleo superfoods actively work to calm that inflammation.

THEY CONTAIN HIGH-QUALITY, EASILY DIGESTIBLE PROTEIN.

That protein helps build and repair muscle to keep you lean and strong. Protein also keeps your blood sugar stable and supplies steady energy to fuel even the most intense workouts (see A Note About Physical Activity, opposite). And protein helps curb cravings for the carbs and sweets that don't do your health any favors. If you're trying to lose weight, high-quality protein is a must with every meal and snack—it will help you to feel full longer so you don't get ravenous and want to eat everything in sight.

THEY ARE GOOD FOR YOUR BONES.

Many people starting Paleo are worried about getting enough calcium because they're not consuming dairy products anymore. But many of these Paleo superfoods provide good amounts of calcium and other bone-strengthening nutrients, such as vitamins D and K, magnesium, potassium, and phosphorus—sometimes even more than you'd find in a glass of milk!

THEY ARE RICH IN FIBER.

Some people are concerned that if they cut out grains, they won't get enough fiber and will miss out on its benefits. But the plant foods in this book contain plenty of fiber to help you reach the 38 grams daily for men and 25 grams daily for women that the Institute of Medicine recommends. That's more than enough fiber—and healthy carbohydrates—to keep your blood sugar steady, lower your cholesterol, and keep you regular, among other benefits. (In fact, if you're new to the Paleo diet and its high fiber content, be sure to drink plenty of water to help ease the transition and avoid constipation.)

THEY ARE NATURAL DETOXIFIERS.

Although our Paleolithic ancestors didn't need to worry about additives and toxins in their food, their personal care products, and the environment, we do; no matter how careful we are in buying high-quality food and products, exposure to toxins is inevitable. That makes it critical to consume the Paleo superfoods that help support your body's natural ability to detoxify.

A NOTE ABOUT PHYSICAL ACTIVITY

Our Paleolithic ancestors lived very active lives, expending a tremendous amount of energy to hunt and gather the food they needed. That daily exercise contributed significantly to their good health, and it's something we need to consider today as well. That's partly why so many Paleo followers have also adopted CrossFit or other intense exercise regimens, and it's why we talk about a Paleo lifestyle, not just a Paleo diet. The combination can be life-changing—I know it was for me!

1
PALEO SUPER PROTEINS

It's hard to overstate the importance of protein in a healthy diet. In fact, the word *protein* comes from the Greek word *proteos*, which means "primary" or "take first place," indicating its significance. Not only does protein provide you with long-lasting energy to help you feel your very best, but also many of your body's functions depend on this vital nutrient. When you eat a protein-containing food, your body breaks it down into amino acids to build, repair, and maintain the cells and tissues in every part of your body. Those amino acids later act like building blocks to build and replenish protein. Proteins also help carry the oxygen in blood and transport fat and cholesterol throughout the body.

Because protein is so critical, it's important to get enough every day—your body can't store it like it does fat. But how much do you need? The Institute of Medicine has established a Recommended Daily Allowance (RDA) that takes into account age and gender differences.

RECOMMENDED DIETARY ALLOWANCE FOR PROTEIN

Grams of protein needed each day

Children ages 1–3	13
Children ages 4–8	19
Children ages 9–13	34
Girls ages 14–18	46
Boys ages 14–18	52
Women ages 19–70+	46
Men ages 19–70+	56

One thing this chart doesn't take into consideration, however, is the quality of the protein. There are twenty amino acids, including several you can only get from food, and not all foods contain all the amino acids (or at least, not in high enough amounts to satisfy your requirements). Animal-based foods such as meat, eggs, and fish—foods that we are often encouraged to shun, or at least limit (with the exception of salmon)—are complete, or high-quality, proteins because they provide all of the essential amino acids. To be called a Paleo superfood, the protein also must be highly bioavailable, meaning your body can readily use it. The closer you can get those animal foods to their original, natural form, the higher quality and more bioavailable the protein is, which is why choosing pasture-raised, organic meats and eggs and wild-caught fish is so important.

SALMON

Salmon may have built its reputation on being a stellar source of omega-3s, but this cold-water fish is also a protein powerhouse—a formidable combination that makes it a true Paleo superfood.

Salmon's high-quality protein includes all the essential amino acids required by the body for growth and maintenance of muscle tissue, which makes your workouts more effective (and makes you feel less sore the next day!). It also helps keep your metabolism humming even after you've finished exercising, making it a good choice if you're watching your weight.

The American Heart Association recommends that adults eat at least two servings of salmon or other fish high in omega-3 fatty acids per week. But does it matter whether you choose wild-caught or farm-raised salmon? Our ancestors ate only wild-caught salmon, and here's why contemporary Paleo followers should, too: one 4-ounce (112 g) serving of wild-caught salmon provides more than 2 grams of omega-3s and 29.1 grams of protein—33 percent and 20 percent more than farm-raised varieties, respectively.

There is also some concern about the practice of salmon farming, including contamination with PCBs (polychlorinated biphenyls), an environmental toxin that can disrupt the endocrine system and damage the nervous system. Because farmed salmon are raised in crowded pens, which generate a large amount of waste and pollutants, the fish are fed antibiotics to protect them against disease and infection. The fish meal they eat (likely the source of those PCBs) is also filled with artificial coloring to allow the fish to achieve the peach-colored flesh that we have come to associate with salmon. Wild-caught salmon achieve their color naturally by consuming carotenoid-rich krill in their natural environments.

In addition, farmed salmon are lower in protein and fattier because they do not swim long distances, and they are higher in saturated fats compared with their wild counterparts. While they do provide omega-3s, they also contain a significantly higher amount of omega-6 fatty acids (consuming too many omega-6s can trigger inflammation).

Given the concerns about farm-raised fish, I recommend choosing wild-caught salmon whenever possible. When you shop, look for an indication that the salmon is wild-caught from Alaska—both the Marine Stewardship Council and the Monterey Bay Aquarium Seafood Watch consider this an excellent, sustainable choice. Wild-caught salmon from Washington, Oregon, and California are rated good alternatives as well. And keep in mind that salmon labeled Atlantic or Norwegian are almost always farm-raised.

OMEGA-3 SPOTLIGHT

A primary emphasis of the Paleo lifestyle is achieving a healthy ratio (ideally 2:1, or even 1:1) of omega-6s to omega-3s. Salmon's exceptionally high omega-3 content helps you achieve that ratio and earns it a solid place on the Paleo superfood list. Studies show that omega-3s, especially the fatty acids docosahexaenoic acid (DHA) and eicosapentaenoic acid (EPA), provide some extraordinary health benefits.

REDUCED INFLAMMATION

Inflammation can wreak havoc on your body, contributing to numerous health problems and accelerating the aging process. But even in small amounts, the omega-3s found in salmon reduce the body's production of prostaglandins, powerful hormone-like substances that can cause excessive inflammation. In particular, research shows that omega-3s can improve inflammatory conditions such as heart disease (see below), rheumatoid arthritis, and asthma, and they may even help prevent cancer, although more studies are needed.

A HEALTHIER HEART

Omega-3s protect your heart in several ways. Inflammation damages the delicate cells that form the lining inside arteries, which in turn leads to plaque buildup and greater risk of heart attack. In fact, a study published in the *Journal of the American Medical Association* found that women who ate as little as one serving per week of fish containing omega-3s could reduce their risk of cardiac arrest by 50 percent. And Japanese research found that people who ate fish rich in omega-3s every day showed a 56 percent lower risk of heart attack and 37 percent lower risk of heart disease compared with occasional eaters.

BETTER BRAIN FUNCTION

Omega-3s boast significant brain benefits. A 2007 study in *Alternative Medicine Review* noted that DHA is critical for brain development, while EPA has more impact on mood, and supplementing with a combination of the two improves both depression and cognitive function. A 2013 study in *Ageing Research Reviews* suggests that dietary intake of omega-3s protects your brain from age-related cognitive decline by bolstering your brain's own repair mechanisms, buffering against stress, and improving nerve formation and nervous system communication.

A TRIMMER WAISTLINE

Surprisingly, eating more of these healthy fats can switch on your body's natural weight-control devices and help you slim down. By boosting insulin's effectiveness, omega-3s improve blood sugar control, which helps reduce food cravings and overeating. Omega-3s stimulate the secretion of leptin, a hormone produced by fat cells that suppresses appetite and burns stored fat so you can drop pounds while maintaining muscle (which is, after all, what you want!). Omega-3s also help your body to burn off calories before they get stored as fat and reduce cellular inflammation, a condition that promotes weight gain.

SHOPPING FOR SALMON

There are several varieties of salmon, each of which has a slightly different nutritional and flavor profile.

CHINOOK (KING SALMON): The largest of the Pacific salmon, considered by many to be the best tasting. Its flesh can range from deep red to almost white. Omega-3 content per 4-ounce (112 g) serving: 2.1 grams.

SOCKEYE: It has a deeper red–colored flesh and the second-highest fat content. It is a full-flavored, strong-tasting fish and is often canned. Omega-3 content: 1.5 grams.

COHO: With a bright red flesh and a slightly more delicate texture than king salmon (but a similar flavor), it has less fat than king or sockeye salmon. Omega-3 content: 1.3 grams.

PINK SALMON (HUMPBACK): The most common of the Pacific salmon. They are very light in flesh color, have a blander flavor than other salmon varieties, and are usually canned. Omega-3 content: 1.5 grams.

CHUM (DOG SALMON): Its firm, coarse flesh is pale in color and has a lower fat content than other salmon. It's mostly used for smoked salmon and canning. Omega-3 content: 1 gram.

SIMPLY GRILLED SALMON OVER SUMMER SALAD

Salmon is high in protein and omega-3 fatty acids, which are essential for heart health. Plus, it's delicious. I love this salmon recipe because it's easy to prepare and it pairs well with so many things. You can easily make it for lunch or dinner—one of my favorite lunchtime ideas is to serve this salmon over a seasonal salad, especially in summer with all its wonderful fresh produce.

FOR SALMON:

2 wild-caught salmon fillets (about 1 pound [454 g])

¼ cup (60 ml) fresh lemon juice (about 1 lemon)

¼ cup (60 ml) extra-virgin olive oil

1 teaspoon dried basil

1 teaspoon dried oregano

½ teaspoon dried rosemary

1 teaspoon minced garlic

½ teaspoon sea salt

¼ teaspoon freshly ground black pepper

FOR SALAD:

4 cups (280 g) organic mixed greens

1 large peach, cut into small pieces

⅓ cup (42 g) fresh raspberries

½ cup (65 g) carrot sticks

½ cup (60 g) sliced and quartered zucchini

FOR DRESSING:

3 tablespoons (45 ml) extra-virgin olive oil

1 tablespoon (15 ml) white balsamic vinegar

Juice from ½ lemon

Freshly ground black pepper to taste

To make the salmon: Wash the salmon fillets and pat dry with paper towels. Place into a large resealable plastic bag. In a medium bowl, combine the lemon juice, olive oil, basil, oregano, rosemary, garlic, salt, and pepper. Whisk together until well incorporated. Pour the marinade into the bag with the salmon and seal. Let the salmon marinate for 1 hour in the refrigerator.

Heat a grill pan over medium-high heat. Add the salmon and grill on both sides until cooked through or to how you prefer your salmon (about 3 to 4 minutes on each side, depending on how thick the salmon is).

To make the salad: In a large bowl, add the mixed greens, peach, raspberries, carrot, and zucchini. Toss well.

To make the dressing: In a small bowl, whisk together the olive oil, white balsamic vinegar, and lemon juice. Add ground black pepper to taste.

Divide the salad between 2 plates, drizzle the dressing over the salad and top with the salmon or serve on the side. Enjoy!

MAKES 2 SERVINGS

EGGS

Humans have enjoyed eggs—one of nature's most perfect foods—for centuries. A single egg is packed with 6 grams of high-quality protein and includes all the amino acids (the building blocks of protein) the body needs. If you're watching your weight, eggs are a great choice—not only does their protein help you meet the Paleo goal of preserving and building lean muscle, but it also creates a feeling of fullness, which can help curb cravings. And if it's protein you are after, don't rely on the whites alone. While the white supplies a little more than half of an egg's protein (as well as magnesium and potassium, nutrients that help your muscles and nerves function properly and improve cardiovascular health, according to the National Institutes of Health) the yolk boasts some impressive nutritional stats as well.

Egg yolks are one of the few natural food sources of vitamin D—one yolk provides 10 percent of the daily value. Vitamin D helps your body absorb calcium to keep your bones strong, and it plays many other roles in your body, including supporting your immune system. The yolks are also the most concentrated source of choline in our diets, notes a 2009 study in *Nutrition Reviews*. Choline is critical for memory and brain function as well as liver function, and it helps your nerves communicate with your muscles. Egg yolks also provide nearly all of eggs' vitamin A, several B vitamins, iron, cholesterol, and selenium.

THE CHOLESTEROL CONUNDRUM

But what about all that awful cholesterol, you ask? We have been scared away from some wonderful, nutrient-dense foods by media and marketing hype that speculated about the effects of dietary fat and cholesterol on human health. For many years, folks have been removing eggs (or at least the yolks) entirely from their diets, afraid that consuming cholesterol would increase their risk of heart disease. That's why you won't find eggs on many other superfood lists.

But it turns out that eating cholesterol doesn't actually raise the cholesterol levels in your blood much at all. In fact, a review published in *Current Opinion in Clinical Nutrition and Metabolic Care* found that eating eggs has no discernible impact on blood cholesterol levels in about 70 percent of the population. In the remaining 30 percent who are especially sensitive, consuming dietary cholesterol does increase harmful LDL cholesterol. However, it also boosts beneficial HDL cholesterol, maintaining a healthy ratio that does not raise the risk of cardiovascular disease.

So if you have normal cholesterol levels, eating a whole egg a day should not adversely affect your health. In fact, cholesterol is actually essential to a healthy brain and body. For example, cholesterol is the precursor molecule in our bodies from which all of our hormones are made, which means it's important to consume enough to promote healthy hormone balance. So don't fall for the hype—these little nutrient powerhouses absolutely qualify as a Paleo superfood.

WHAT MAKES A BETTER EGG?

You've probably seen eggs labeled "organic," "cage-free," or "free-range" at the supermarket. While these are better choices than conventional eggs, those labels don't necessarily mean the eggs are the same quality and have the same nutrient profile as eggs from chickens raised on pasture. Confusing, huh? Here's how to "crack" the carton codes, along with tips for making the best choice.

BEST: The pasture is where the chickens get access to grass, worms, bugs, and sunshine, all of which improve the quality of their eggs so they are chock-full of healthy nutrients—and it's how chickens were raised for thousands of years, up until the advent of industrial agriculture. Pasture-raised eggs from your local farmer or market are the gold standard.

BETTER: Free-range chickens have access to the outdoors at least 51 percent of the time. Unfortunately, "access to outdoors" may only be a tiny 2-foot by 2-foot (61 x 61 cm) opening leading to a concrete slab outside with no pasture. And while ruminant animals like cows are not allowed in the chickens' feedlots, there are no restrictions regarding what the chickens are fed.

BETTER: *Organic* is a term that is defined by the U.S. Department of Agriculture (USDA). Hens laying organic eggs have little to no exposure to pesticides, herbicides, and commercial fertilizers, and they don't receive hormones or antibiotics unless they get ill. They consume organic feed, and they might have outdoor access but may not use it. Animals are not necessarily grass-fed. Certification is costly, and some reputable farms are forced to forego it.

GOOD: Cage-free hens are able to freely roam an enclosed area with unlimited access to food and fresh water. They're allowed perches and nest boxes to lay their eggs, but in larger farms the hens may be packed in pretty tightly (tens of thousands of hens in one big barn). Additionally, there are no standards or auditing to ensure cage-free compliance.

EGGS: NATURE'S MULTIVITAMIN

Eggs are packed with health-promoting nutrients. Here are just a few of the reasons why eggs should be a mainstay of a Paleo diet.

- **GROWTH:** The protein in eggs helps your body repair and make new cells. Eggs are an excellent source of B vitamins, which help nerve and blood cells work properly and help make DNA. Vitamin B_6 is particularly important for brain development during pregnancy and infancy. Eggs also provide good quantities of vitamin A, which is essential for normal growth and development.

- **HEART HEALTH:** The vitamin E in eggs protects against heart disease (and some cancers). Magnesium helps keep heart rhythm steady and regulates blood pressure.

- **BONE HEALTH:** Eggs contain vitamin D, which promotes mineral absorption and good bone health. The yolks provide phosphorus, essential for healthy bones and teeth. Magnesium boosts bone strength.

- **THYROID HEALTH:** Your body needs the iodine in eggs to make thyroid hormones. Eggs are also a very good source of selenium, which helps regulate thyroid function.

- **EYE HEALTH:** Eggs are rich in the antioxidants lutein and zeaxanthin, which reduce the risk of developing macular degeneration and cataracts.

BAKED EGG CUPS WITH TOMATOES, SPINACH, AND PROSCIUTTO

The beauty of these protein-packed baked egg cups is that they are very simple to put together, and they don't require an exact ingredient list. Once you have the essentials you can experiment with whatever you have around the house, making every breakfast with these cups different and fun.

½ teaspoon coconut oil or ghee

2 cups (60 g) spinach leaves, chopped

⅓ cup (50 g) cherry tomatoes, halved

1 clove garlic, minced

4 slices prosciutto

1 to 2 tablespoons (15 to 30 ml) Spinach Basil Walnut Pesto (page 52), plus more for serving

4 pasture-raised eggs

Sea salt and freshly ground black pepper to taste

Chopped basil, for serving (optional)

Preheat the oven to 350°F (180°C, or gas mark 4).

In a skillet over medium heat, melt the coconut oil. Add the chopped spinach, cherry tomatoes, and garlic and stir. Continue to sauté the spinach and tomatoes until the spinach has wilted down and the tomatoes are soft, about 1 to 2 minutes.

Line each of 4 ramekins with 1 slice prosciutto. Divide the spinach and tomato mixture equally among the ramekins, and then top each with a dollop of pesto. Finally, crack an egg into each. Season the tops with a little sea salt and freshly ground pepper. Place the ramekins on a baking sheet and bake for 20 minutes, until egg yolk has set. Serve with an additional dollop of pesto or freshly chopped basil.

These are best enjoyed the day you make them, but they can be stored in the refrigerator, covered, and reheated the next day.

MAKES 4 SERVINGS

GRASS-FED ORGANIC BEEF

Nutrition experts have long recommended limiting your red meat consumption. And if you're talking about conventionally raised beef, they're probably correct. Yes, beef is an excellent source of protein, which our bodies need for repairing tissue, preserving lean muscle, and boosting energy. And the protein it provides is bioavailable, meaning your body can easily digest and absorb it. Beef also offers impressive amounts of vitamins A, B_6, B_{12}, D, and E and minerals (including iron, zinc, and selenium) that are all necessary for optimum health. But grass-fed beef has a nutritional edge over conventional beef (not to mention its environmental advantages—see sidebar): grass-fed beef contains more omega-3 fatty acids, vitamins A and E, antioxidants, and a special type of fat called conjugated linoleic acid (CLA) than its conventional counterpart.

Grass-fed organic beef is the best choice for a Paleo diet. All foods eaten by hunter-gathers are more or less wild, grown with little or no human interference, with no additives, hormones, antibiotics, or chemicals. One hundred percent grass-fed and finished cows are allowed to graze on their natural food source their entire lives, and organic cattle do not receive antibiotics or growth hormones. They eat organic feed and they have access to the outdoors. You can find 100 percent grass-fed organic beef at well-stocked natural food stores, but keep in mind that smaller farms that raise grass-fed livestock may not go to the trouble (and expense) to be certified organic, even though many of them follow organic practices. If you buy your meat at a farmers' market or through a community-supported agriculture (CSA) program, ask how the animals are raised and finished. See Resources (page 214) for help in locating a supplier.

THE SKINNY ON FAT

Conventionally raised cows are fed grains, corn, and soy to fatten them up quickly so they're less expensive to produce. Grass-fed cattle graze on pasture, and they get more exercise doing it, which means their meat is leaner. It also means that what fat is in the

ENVIRONMENTAL IMPACT

Choosing grass-fed organic beef not only benefits your health, but it's also better for the health of the planet. Conventional cattle farming relies heavily on fossil fuels to produce the grain-based feed, antibiotics, and hormones the cows receive, as well as the chemical fertilizers used on the land. Organically raised pastured animals, on the other hand, eat naturally growing grass and actually fertilize the land they graze on. In addition, growing grass in a field prevents soil erosion, requires less irrigation, and removes carbon dioxide from the atmosphere more effectively than any other crop.

meat has a healthier profile: less artery-clogging saturated fat and inflammatory omega-6s, and more omega-3s and CLA.

Omega-3s and -6s are polyunsaturated fats (see sidebar) that your body needs, but in balance. Our modern diets are almost always too high in omega-6 fatty acids, which can trigger inflammation. Over time, inflammation can lead to all kinds of diseases and health problems, including heart disease, digestive problems, obesity, and diabetes. Omega-3 fatty acids work to calm that inflammation, which is why study after study has found that omega-3s are so beneficial to our health. But most of us just don't get enough. In fact, a 2010 study in *Nutrition Journal* noted that the typical American diet contains up to thirty times more omega-6s than omega-3s—a far cry from the ideal ratio of 2:1 that the Paleo diet recommends. Grass-fed beef provides the omegas in almost exactly that ratio (on average, conventional beef has a ratio of 8:1), which is one more reason why it's a Paleo superfood.

CLA is another surprisingly beneficial type of fat. According to a 2012 study in *Critical Reviews in Food Science and Nutrition*, CLA promotes the development of lean muscle tissue and reduces body fat, lowers the risk of cardiovascular diseases and cancer, regulates immune and inflammatory responses, and even improves bone mass. Beef is a major dietary source of CLA, and grass-fed organic beef provides up to twice the amount you'll find in conventional beef.

FIRE UP THE GRILL

Grass-fed beef has a different taste and texture than grain-fed beef, which also affects how you cook it. Grass-fed beef has a richer flavor that can vary a bit depending on the time of year and where the animal has grazed. And because a grass-fed animal has to walk around and forage for its meal, the meat can sometimes be slightly less tender than what most folks are used to eating. But because it's leaner, grass-fed beef doesn't leave you with that rock-in-your-gut feeling after eating it.

THE FAMILY OF FATS

Fats are a complex bunch, so to make it less confusing, let's picture them as a family tree. At the top, there are two parents: saturated and unsaturated fats. Saturated fat is packed with hydrogen atoms, making it solid at room temperature. The family of unsaturated fats (which are liquid at room temp) includes two children: monounsaturated and polyunsaturated. In the polyunsaturated family, you'll find omega-6 and omega-3 fatty acids. While omega-3s have garnered most of the headlines, each type of fat, eaten in appropriate amounts, can contribute to your health.

Omega-3 and omega-6 fatty acids both use the same enzymes and transport systems to produce biochemicals in our body, so the presence of one greatly affects the behavior of the other. When you consume high amounts of omega-6 fats, your body creates inflammatory compounds, and fewer enzymes are available for omega-3s to balance them out with anti-inflammatory agents. In general, the Paleo diet aims for a 2:1 (or even 1:1) ratio of omega-6 to omega-3 fats, which approximates the balance that our hunter-gatherer ancestors achieved.

As a general rule, grass-fed beef needs to be cooked slower and at a lower temperature (by about 50°F [10°C]) than grain-fed beef to keep it moist and tender. Try serving it a little rarer than you're used to as well. And always let the meat come to room temperature before cooking—tossing a cold steak or a cold hamburger on the grill often results in an overcooked exterior and a very rare center.

See page 32 for tips on purchasing grass-fed meats.

PALEO VEGGIE AND GRASS-FED BEEF CHILI

Traditional chili is typically made with beans. This Paleo version skips the beans in favor of a variety of vegetables. The vegetables add flavor and extra nutrients, and I guarantee you won't miss the beans. Top the chili with avocado to take it to a whole other level of delicious.

2 tablespoons (28 g) bacon grease or coconut oil

1 small yellow onion, diced

2 small cloves garlic, minced

1 pound (454 g) grass-fed ground beef

2 tablespoons (15 g) chili powder

1½ tablespoons (11 g) paprika

1 tablespoon (7 g) cumin

2 teaspoons dried oregano

½ teaspoon red pepper flakes

½ teaspoon sea salt

¼ teaspoon cayenne pepper

1 zucchini, diced

2 carrots, peeled and diced

1 small sweet potato, peeled and diced

1 can (28-ounces, or 784 g) crushed tomatoes

½ cup (120 ml) low-sodium chicken broth

⅓ cup (5 g) chopped cilantro

1 avocado, diced (optional)

Place a large pot over medium-high heat and melt the bacon grease. Add the diced onion and garlic and sauté for 2 to 3 minutes, or until the onions are translucent. Add the beef and break up into crumbles as it cooks. Cook the beef until it is no longer pink in color, about 3 to 5 minutes. Add the chili powder, paprika, cumin, oregano, red pepper flakes, sea salt, cayenne pepper, diced zucchini, diced carrots, diced sweet potato, can of crushed tomatoes, and chicken broth and stir to combine.

Reduce the heat to low and simmer for 25 to 30 minutes, or until the vegetables are tender. Add the cilantro and stir to incorporate. Serve the chili with diced avocado, if desired.

MAKES 6 TO 8 SERVINGS

QUICK TIP:

If you have too much chili left over, save it for a rainy day by placing it in an air-tight container in the freezer. When you're ready to eat it, remove it from the freezer, defrost, then reheat on the stove until warm. Add the toppings of your choice and serve.

GRASS-FED BISON

Bison (also called buffalo) are the largest land mammals in North America. Grass-fed bison today graze much like their ancestors from prehistoric times, eating nothing but the grass they roam through for the majority of their lives. The nutrient-dense grasses bison eat produce a delicious meat rich in Paleo-critical protein, iron, omega-3s, and vitamin E. With a flavor and texture similar to those of beef, grass-fed bison is outrageously lean compared with grain-fed cattle—a 3-ounce (84 g) bison burger contains 7 grams of fat compared with a traditional beef burger's 15 grams—and its fat is healthier for you because it's higher in omega-3s. Bison is also lower in fat, calories, and cholesterol than skinless chicken or turkey, making it a wonderful protein to incorporate into your Paleo lifestyle.

Another reason why grass-fed bison earns the distinction of being a superfood is its high content of selenium (an essential trace mineral). In fact, grass-fed bison have as much as four times more selenium than grain-fed bison, according to findings from Martin Marchello at the Carrington Research Extension Center at North Dakota State University. Just 3 ounces (84 g) of grass-fed bison provides more than 100 micrograms of selenium (several times the daily requirement), which can help reduce your risk of cancer and may even make you happier: a 1990 study in the journal *Psychopharmacology* found that participants who took a 100-microgram selenium supplement reported substantially better moods after two and a half weeks than participants who received a placebo.

GRASS-FED VERSUS GRAIN-FED

Grass-fed and finished bison delivers nearly three and a half times more omega-3 fatty acids than grain-fed bison, giving it a healthy omega-6 to omega-3 fatty acid ratio of 4:1 or less. When bison eat grains, that ratio can climb to a very unhealthy 20:1, or sometimes even higher. A review published in *Biomedicine & Pharmacotherapy* in 2002 noted that high omega-6 to omega-3 ratios have been linked to cardiovascular disease, inflammatory and autoimmune diseases such as asthma and rheumatoid arthritis, and cancer, among other health problems. And keep in mind that even meat labeled grass-fed can mean that the animals ate grass for most of their lives, but in the last few months they may have been fed grain to fatten them up quickly. Look for 100 percent grass-fed *and finished* meats to make sure the animals ate only their natural diet of nutrient-rich grasses.

Why does what the animals eat matter so much? In hunter-gatherer times, more than 10,000 years ago, grain consumption was perhaps incidental at best—both for humans and the animals we ate. Partly for that reason, our omega-6 to omega-3 ratio in those times was closer to the ideal ratio of 2:1, or even 1:1. Our bodies are extremely well adapted to eating grass-fed animals because until quite recently, that's all that was available to us. Returning to our original diet of grass-fed animals is simply more in line with our physiology.

PURCHASING AND PREPARING BISON

As with other grass-fed proteins, the best way to find out about the diet and care of the animals is to ask the farmer directly about the grass-fed bison you are purchasing.

Grass-fed bison meat tastes like beef, with a slightly sweeter and richer flavor (note that you won't get this delicious taste from feedlot or grain-finished bison). Bison is naturally flavorful and tender and can be prepared much the same as beef, although 100 percent grass-fed bison meat requires about one-third less cooking time. But don't be in a hurry! Cooking grass-fed bison for longer time over a lower temperature will help maintain its moist and tender texture.

HOW RAISING GRASS-FED MEAT BENEFITS THE ENVIRONMENT

In recent years, many news outlets have reported that vegetarian or vegan diets are healthier for the planet. That may be true—if you're comparing those diets to industrial livestock farming, which uses high amounts of fossil fuels, produces more greenhouse gasses than all of our modes of transportation combined, and contributes to land degradation and air and water pollution, according to the Food and Agriculture Organization of the United Nations. But when you consider grass-fed animals, history tells a different story.

Roaming herds of grazing animals actually support the land they eat from. They eat up the old growth, aerate the soil, spread grass seeds with their movements, and fertilize the soil with their manure. The deeply rooted grass holds moisture in the soil and prevents erosion, keeping the land healthy so it doesn't require chemical fertilizers, pesticides, or irrigation. This rich soil can then support additional grazing or another food crop. The animals can also graze on land that is unsuitable for growing other crops, making livestock a good option for those with rocky or sloping land.

MUSHROOM GARLIC HERB BISON BURGER

Also known as buffalo, bison tends to be leaner than beef, yet it's just as flavorful. In addition to packing in more than 20 grams of protein per 4-ounce (113 g) serving, ground bison contains more iron per serving than ground beef, chicken, or pork. In this recipe, mixing the grass-fed bison with mushrooms makes for an extra-juicy burger, and the herbs provide a delicious punch of flavor.

7 ounces (196 g) button mushrooms

⅓ cup (55 g) finely chopped red onion

3 cloves garlic, minced

1 pound (454 g) ground grass-fed bison

½ teaspoon sea salt

½ teaspoon black pepper

1 tablespoon (1 g) chopped parsley

1½ teaspoons minced fresh rosemary

1½ teaspoons minced fresh sage

1 teaspoon fresh thyme leaves

1 cup (70 g) baby arugula

1 large tomato, cut into 8 thin slices

In the bowl of a food processor, process the mushrooms until minced. Transfer to a large mixing bowl and add the chopped onion and minced garlic and toss to combine. Then add the bison, salt, pepper, parsley, rosemary, sage, and thyme leaves. With hands (or a fork), mix until well combined and form into four ¾-inch (2 cm) thick patties; cover and set aside. Let the burgers come to room temperature to help keep them juicy and allow the flavors to blend.

Heat a grill (or grill pan) over medium heat. Add the bison patties and cook for 5 minutes on one side; turn and cook for 4 more minutes.

Divide the arugula evenly among 4 plates, then top each with 2 tomato slices and a burger. These burgers are best enjoyed immediately but you can reheat them the next day as well.

MAKES 4 SERVINGS

GRASS-FED LAMB

A central feature of a hunter-gatherer-type lifestyle is eating high-quality, unprocessed animal protein, such as that in lamb and other lean, organic, grass-fed meat. Considered a red meat, grass-fed lamb offers health benefits similar to those found in grass-fed beef. For example, delicious and tender lamb is one of the richest sources of easily digestible protein: a 3-ounce (84 g) serving provides about 24 grams of protein. And grass-fed lamb offers about 8 percent more protein than meat from grain-fed lambs. This high-quality protein helps build and maintain muscle (especially important to combat the natural muscle loss that comes with aging) and is a readily available source of energy, so it is an ideal fuel for even the most intense workouts. That protein also keeps your blood sugar levels steady and helps you feel full longer, which can help combat cravings and make it easier to reach or stay at a healthy weight. One difference between lamb and other red meats: because lamb is less allergenic, most people do not experience adverse food sensitivity reactions to lamb as they may to beef (or poultry, for that matter).

Grass-fed lamb is rich in vitamin B_{12} and selenium, nutrients that are important for heart health. Vitamin B_{12} helps regulate levels of homocysteine, an amino acid linked to cardiovascular disease, making it less likely to damage artery walls and form dangerous blood clots. A 2012 study published in *Molecular Nutrition and Food Research* noted that having low selenium levels is linked to a higher risk of heart disease, possibly because selenium acts as a powerful antioxidant to protect blood vessels from free radical damage.

Lamb is also a great source of zinc, which helps keep your immune system in top shape. Low levels of zinc significantly hamper your immune system's ability to respond to threats, noted researchers from Oregon State University in a 2012 study. That makes you more susceptible to everything from the common cold to serious infections such as staph. Not getting enough zinc also puts you at risk for low-grade chronic inflammation, which can lead to all kinds of health problems, including asthma, cardiovascular disease, and accelerated aging. Zinc-rich foods such as lamb contribute to the Paleo diet's effectiveness at combating that inflammation.

WHY GRASS-FED?

As with beef and bison, grass-fed lambs are eating the way nature intended, which makes them the best choice for a Paleo diet. Because the animals are eating the nutrient-rich grasses their bodies were designed to eat and they have to travel long distances to get their food, they are lean and healthy. But even though lambs grazing on pasture have 14 percent less fat than their grain-fed counterparts, the meat boasts higher levels of healthy fats such as conjugated linoleic acid and omega-3 fatty acids. In fact, 60 percent of the fat in grass is a type of omega-3 fat called alpha-linolenic acid. Eating just three servings of grass-fed red meat such as beef or lamb per week can significantly raise your body's levels of omega-3s, according to a 2011 study in the *British Journal of Nutrition*. That will get you closer to the Paleo ideal ratio of 2:1 (or 1:1) of omega-6s to omega-3s. Both omega-3s and conjugated linoleic acid help calm inflammation and may reduce your risk for heart disease, among other benefits. Grass-fed lamb also offers more of the antioxidants vitamin E and beta-carotene than grain-fed meat. Clearly, grass-fed is the way to go.

COOKING TIPS

Lamb just might be the most flavorful of all the meats, which could explain why it is a staple in cuisines throughout the world, including New Zealand, Australia, and the countries of the Middle East and the Mediterranean. Keep in mind that lamb can easily be overcooked and become dry—I recommend using cooking methods that will keep it moist and tender, such as braising. And be sure to watch your cooking times. Different cuts of lamb lend themselves well to different cooking techniques. Use the following as a guideline.

SHOULDER: Best used to make stew and cooked to medium-well.

SHANK/BREAST: Best braised and cooked to well done.

LEG: Best roasted and cooked to well done.

LOIN (LAMB CHOP): Best broiled and cooked to medium-well.

RACK OF LAMB: Best roasted or broiled to medium-rare.

GROUND LAMB: Best sautéed and cooked to well done.

SHOPPING "GRASS-FED"

Unfortunately, the grass-fed label doesn't tell you anything about whether the animals were given antibiotics or hormones, or if they were treated with or were around chemical pesticides, according to the U.S. Department of Agriculture. Your best option is to buy grass-fed meat from a farmer who can tell you how he treats and finishes his animals, or through a market that can tell you how the meat is produced. See Resources (page 214) for help in locating a direct source for grass-fed lamb. The next best thing is to look for a third-party certification. Here are some common ones:

AMERICAN GRASS-FED CERTIFICATION: Considered the best third-party certification; verifies that the animals ate only grass and forage for their entire lives, were raised on pasture and not confined to feedlots, and were never treated with antibiotics or growth hormones.

CERTIFIED HUMANE RAISED AND HANDLED: Meets the Humane Farm Animal Care program standards, which include feeding the animals a nutritious diet without antibiotics or hormones and raising them with shelter, resting areas, sufficient space, and the ability to engage in natural behaviors.

ANIMAL WELFARE APPROVED: Species-specific welfare standards that ensure the animals are raised on pasture or range, are allowed to behave naturally, and are in a state of physical and psychological well-being. For lamb, the standards prohibit growth hormones and discourage the use of antibiotics.

USDA ORGANIC (LIVESTOCK): Producers must meet animal health and welfare standards, avoid antibiotics or growth hormones, use 100 percent organic feed (may include grains or soy), and provide animals with access to the outdoors.

ROSEMARY LAMB CHOPS

Fresh herbs brighten the flavor of these lamb chops and highlight the smokiness of the grill—plus they provide antioxidants. This mouthwatering main dish is perfect for entertaining friends or serving as a weeknight dinner for the family.

To make the lamb chops: Preheat the grill to medium-high heat, 350° to 400°F (180° to 200°C).

Place lamb chops in a large bowl and drizzle with the olive oil. In a small bowl, mix the rosemary and thyme and toss with your fingers. Add the garlic, coriander, sea salt, and pepper and stir to combine. Sprinkle the herb mixture over the lamb chops and toss to coat the chops well. Let stand for 30 minutes.

Grill lamb chops on the grill rack, covered with the grill lid, for 3 to 4 minutes on each side for medium-rare or 8 minutes on each side for medium. Remove from the grill; let stand for 5 minutes.

To make the basil chimichurri sauce: Combine all the ingredients in a bowl and stir well. Serve with the lamb chops.

MAKES 4 SERVINGS, ¾ CUP (160 G) SAUCE

MAKE A MEAL OUT OF IT

Looking for a great side dish to go along with these lamb chops? Try pairing with Roasted Lemon Sage Carrots and Parsnips (page 96) or Roasted Broccoli and Cauliflower with Garlic and Lemon (page 188).

FOR LAMB CHOPS:

8 lamb rib chops, 1 inch (2.5 cm) thick

1 tablespoon (15 ml) extra-virgin olive oil

2 tablespoons (3 g) fresh rosemary, chopped

1 tablespoon (2.5 g) fresh thyme, chopped

2 cloves garlic, minced

½ teaspoon ground coriander

½ teaspoon sea salt

½ teaspoon coarsely ground black pepper

FOR BASIL CHIMICHURRI SAUCE:

½ cup (20 g) finely chopped fresh basil

⅓ cup (80 ml) extra-virgin olive oil

¼ cup (15 g) finely chopped parsley

2 tablespoons (30 ml) apple cider vinegar

½ teaspoon sea salt

½ teaspoon ground cumin

¼ teaspoon ground black pepper

1 clove garlic, minced

SHRIMP

Shrimp may be little, but they offer super-sized nutritional value and health benefits. As a low-calorie, high-protein pick packed with healthy fats, minerals, and antioxidants, these delicious crustaceans are an important component to a balanced Paleo diet.

Our hunter-gatherer ancestors couldn't afford to be tired all the time or they'd miss out on their next meal. The foods they ate—such as shrimp—gave them the energy they needed to survive. Shrimp provide 6 grams of energizing protein per ounce (28 g), so a 3-ounce (84 g) serving provides about one-quarter of your recommended daily allowance—all for only 100 calories. Plus, the iron in shrimp carries revitalizing oxygen throughout your body and helps produce adenosine triphosphate (ATP), your body's natural energy source.

Shrimp are also an excellent source of vitamin B_{12}—a 3-ounce (84 g) serving provides more than half of your daily requirement. Vitamin B_{12} helps form red blood cells, keeps your neurological system functioning properly, and helps synthesize DNA. Several large studies show that B_{12} can also reduce levels of homocysteine, a marker of low-grade inflammation that raises your risk for heart disease and stroke.

ANTIOXIDANT DEFENSE

Shrimp contain good amounts of the antioxidant minerals zinc and selenium. Besides fighting age-accelerating free radicals, both minerals support thyroid function and keep your immune system in fighting shape. Zinc is also important for healthy hair and skin, especially wound healing. And selenium shows promise in both reducing your risk of cancer (especially prostate cancer) and slowing its progression, according to a 2008 study in the *Journal of Nutritional Biochemistry*.

But the most abundant antioxidant in shrimp is a carotenoid—a naturally occurring pigment that gives shrimp its vibrant orange-pink color—called astaxanthin. This powerful free radical fighter protects you against inflammation and oxidative damage to your cells, helping prevent health problems ranging from cardiovascular disease to diabetes, cancer, and eye diseases such as cataracts and macular degeneration, according to a 2011 review published in *Molecular Nutrition and Food Research*.

FRIENDLY FATS

Many people shy away from shrimp because they are high in cholesterol (about 180 milligrams in a 3-ounce [84 g] serving). Surprisingly, however, eating saturated fat is more likely to raise your blood cholesterol levels than eating cholesterol itself. Shrimp are naturally low in saturated fat, and a study from researchers at the Rockefeller University found that people with normal cholesterol levels who ate shrimp every day for three weeks maintained a healthy lipid profile, or the ratio of LDL ("bad") cholesterol to HDL ("good") cholesterol that can indicate cardiovascular disease risk. The researchers suggested that the Paleo-prized omega-3 fatty acids in shrimp may also help keep cholesterol levels in check.

Those omega-3s can calm harmful inflammation throughout your body and protect your cardiovascular system in other ways as well. The American Heart Association recommends that most people consume two meals of seafood containing omega-3s per week (about 6 ounces [168 g]). With 0.4 grams of omega-3s per 3-ounce (84 g) serving, shrimp are a super choice to help you meet that goal. And you can feel good about eating shrimp as often as you like because they are also low in mercury and other environmental toxins.

SHOPPING FOR SHRIMP

In keeping with the Paleo principle of eating foods closest to their original source, wild-caught shrimp is the way to go. The Monterey Bay Aquarium's list of sustainable shrimp species names wild-caught Canadian Pacific spot prawns and wild-caught pink shrimp (also called bay shrimp, cocktail shrimp, ocean shrimp, salad shrimp, or ebi) from Oregon as the best choices. Visit www.montereybayaquarium.org to learn more about other good options. If you're buying packaged shrimp, check that the ingredients list only includes shrimp, and possibly salt. Some brands include a chemical called sodium tripolyphosphate (STP) to help the shrimp retain moisture, but it's unnecessary and not natural.

Eat fresh shrimp within a day or two; frozen shrimp will keep for several weeks in the coldest part of your freezer.

TIPS FOR PREPARING SHRIMP:

You can cook shrimp with the shell on or peel them first, depending on how you'll be using them. (Some people recommend always cooking them in the shell because the shell holds a lot of flavor.) If you are shelling frozen shrimp, don't defrost them all the way—they are easier to shell when they're still slightly frozen. There are several ways to remove the shell, but regardless of how you do it, keep your shrimp cold—on ice or in a bowl of ice water—while you work. My method for removing the shell is to pull or pinch off the head (if it's still attached) and legs, then hold the tail and peel the shell away from the body. You can leave the tail on for decorative purposes, if desired. If you are going to devein your shrimp, you can alternatively leave the shell on and use a very sharp knife to cut down the back of the shrimp, about ¼ inch (6 mm) deep. Use the knife or your fingers to remove the vein (actually the shrimp's digestive tract) or hold it under running water to rinse it out. You can also use an inexpensive shrimp deveiner to do this task.

SOUTHWEST SHRIMP CAKES

These shrimp cakes make for a quick and delicious meal. If you like a little spice, add a kick with red pepper flakes or diced jalapeño. I highly recommend serving these with fresh guacamole—the avocado adds not only more healthy fats, but potassium, fiber, and a wealth of antioxidant vitamins and minerals.

1 pound (454 g) raw wild-caught shrimp, peeled and deveined

½ cup (75 g) finely chopped red bell pepper

2 scallions, chopped

2 tablespoons (2 g) fresh cilantro, chopped

1 clove garlic, minced

3 to 4 teaspoons (7 to 9 g) coconut flour* or 1 tablespoon (7 g) almond flour

2 eggs, beaten

¼ teaspoon sea salt

¼ teaspoon freshly ground black pepper

2 teaspoons coconut oil

*See Resources, page 214.

Chop or dice the shrimp into bite-size pieces. In a large bowl, combine the shrimp, bell pepper, scallions, cilantro, garlic, flour, eggs, salt, and black pepper and mix well. Allow the mixture to sit for 1 minute to allow the coconut flour to soak up some of the liquid. The mixture will be wet, but if it is too wet add just enough coconut flour for it to stick together and form patties. Form the shrimp mixture into 6 to 8 evenly-sized cakes.

Meanwhile, add the coconut oil to a nonstick skillet and heat over medium-high heat.

Add the cakes to the heated skillet, making sure not to overcrowd the skillet (cook in two batches if necessary). Allow the cakes to cook for 2 to 3 minutes before flipping. Don't flip too soon or the cakes will break apart. Once they have cooked on one side, carefully flip and allow the cakes to cook on other side until cooked through, another minute or two. Repeat with the remaining cakes. Serve warm.

MAKES 6 TO 8 SHRIMP CAKES

TUNA

Fossil records indicate that tuna has flourished in our oceans for 40 to 60 million years, long before humans were around to eat them! Our Paleolithic ancestors almost certainly fished for tuna, and for good reason. Tuna is an excellent source of protein—a 3-ounce (84 g) serving of yellowfin tuna provides nearly 25 grams. In addition, its protein efficiency ratio (an index of its amino acid profile and bioavailability) is higher than those for beef, pork, chicken, and milk proteins, notes an article in the journal *Comments on Toxicology*. That makes it a prime Paleo choice. Besides protein, tuna offers the minerals selenium, magnesium, and potassium, the B vitamins, and, of course, those powerful omega-3 fatty acids. Here's a look at some of the other reasons why tuna deserves a prominent place in the Paleo diet.

HEAL YOUR HEART

The magnesium and potassium in tuna protect your heart by lowering your blood pressure and keeping your heart rhythm steady, among other ways. Consuming enough of these minerals through foods can reduce your risk of stroke and other forms of cardiovascular disease as well.

Tuna is also a good source of vitamins B_6, B_{12}, and niacin, which may reduce your risk of cardiovascular disease. While there is conflicting evidence regarding whether supplementing with the B vitamins helps your heart (it does seem to lower homocysteine, a marker of inflammation that indicates risk of heart disease, but recent studies haven't found that the lowered homocysteine levels translate to better heart health), increasing your dietary intake does appear beneficial. A 2010 study that looked at the eating habits of nearly 60,000 Japanese adults found that

those who consumed high levels of vitamin B_6 and folate, in particular, were less likely to die from stroke, coronary heart disease, or heart failure.

Omega-3 fatty acids also play a major role in keeping your cardiovascular system healthy. These good fats calm inflammation that can damage your blood vessels and lead to heart disease. Research indicates that they may also decrease triglycerides (high levels of this type of cholesterol are associated with cardio-vascular disease), slow the development of blockage-forming plaques in your blood vessels, decrease your risk of abnormal heartbeats, and lower blood pressure, according to the American Heart Association.

PROTECT YOUR PEEPERS

The omega-3s that the Paleo diet values so highly are also good for your eyes. Research shows that tuna's omega-3 fatty acids can help prevent and treat age-related macular degeneration, one of the leading causes of vision loss for people over fifty. Additional evidence indicates omega-3s can also help relieve dry eye, a common complaint that's often difficult to treat.

PREVENT CANCER

Studies show that a higher intake of the antioxidant mineral selenium is linked to a lower risk of death from cancer, possibly by protecting you against free radical damage and preventing or slowing tumor growth. A recently discovered compound called selenoneine is the major form of selenium in the blood and tissues of tuna. Selenoneine shows a remarkable ability to defend tuna against free radicals, so researchers suspect that selenoneine can also act as an antioxidant in humans who eat tuna, which could protect against cancer as well as other chronic diseases and premature aging, notes a 2010 study in the *World Journal of Biological Chemistry*.

BOOST BRAIN HEALTH

Tuna provides good amounts of several B vitamins, including B_6, B_{12}, and niacin, which may help prevent or delay cognitive decline and Alzheimer's disease by lowering homocysteine levels, notes a 2012 study in the *Journal of Thrombosis and Thrombolysis*.

Omega-3 fatty acids benefit the brain in several ways as well. Besides helping to create new neurons and improve communication between nerve cells, omega-3s calm inflammation and quench harmful free radicals in the brain, and they are linked to several hormones involved in brain function. Evidence suggests that consuming plenty of omega-3s through diet can protect against age-related cognitive decline and dementia, notes a 2013 study in *Ageing Research Reviews*. Two types of omega-3s, DHA and EPA, might also help combat stress and lift your mood.

WHICH TUNA IS TOPS?

From a sustainability standpoint, the Monterey Bay Aquarium Seafood Watch list's "best choices" are troll- or pole-and-line-caught varieties, including albacore tuna from the United States or Canadian Pacific, bigeye tuna from the U.S. Atlantic, yellowfin from the U.S. Atlantic or Pacific, and skipjack caught worldwide. If you're purchasing canned tuna, you'll want to read the labels closely—look for an indication that it is troll- or pole-and-line-caught (or has the Marine Stewardship Council's blue "Certified Sustainable Seafood" label), that the can does not contain the harmful chemical bisphenol-A (BPA), and if you're buying light tuna, that the fish is skipjack, which is lower in mercury than the yellowfin tuna sometimes found in cans.

A NOTE ABOUT MERCURY

Nearly all fish and shellfish contain traces of mercury, which can harm the developing nervous system of unborn babies and young children, leading to problems with hearing and learning. While most people don't need to worry about consuming too much mercury through the fish and shellfish they eat, the Food and Drug Administration (FDA) and the Environmental Protection Agency (EPA) recommend that women who may become pregnant, pregnant women, nursing mothers, and young children avoid some types of fish and eat fish and shellfish that are lower in mercury. That includes up to 12 ounces (336 g) per week of canned light tuna, or 6 ounces (168 g) per week of canned white (albacore) tuna.

SEARED TUNA WITH TROPICAL SALSA

This tropical salsa adds a delicious dose of vitamin C (from the fruits) and healthy fats (from the avocado) to the tuna's already impressive amounts of vitamins, minerals, and omega-3s. This dish works great as an appetizer because the tuna cooks in minutes and the salsa can be prepared the day before, making it a quick fix to keep your guests happy.

FOR TUNA:

8 to 9 ounces (224 to 252 g) fresh tuna fillet

1 tablespoon (14 g) coconut oil

Sea salt

Freshly ground black pepper

FOR TROPICAL SALSA:

¼ cup (40 g) finely diced fresh pineapple

¼ cup (45 g) finely diced fresh mango

¼ cup (45 g) finely diced fresh kiwi

4 scallions, thinly sliced

2 tablespoons (30 ml) fresh lime juice (about 2 to 3 limes)

1 clove garlic, minced

1 small avocado, peeled, pitted, and finely diced

⅓ cup (5 g) fresh cilantro, coarsely chopped, plus more for garnish

To make the tuna: Cut the tuna into long, fat, square strips or logs about 1 to 1½ inches (2.5 to 3.8 cm) thick. Coat the tuna with the coconut oil and season lightly with sea salt and fresh pepper. Set a 10-inch (25 cm) skillet over high heat. After about 2 to 3 minutes, when the pan is very hot, sear the tuna logs for 20 to 30 seconds on each side. (The goal is to have the tuna seared on the outside and rare on the inside.) Transfer to a clean cutting board and slice into ¼-inch (6 mm) thick pieces.

To make the salsa: Combine the pineapple, mango, kiwi, scallions, lime juice, and garlic in a bowl. Add the avocado and cilantro and gently toss to combine.

To assemble: Place the tuna on a plate and top with a small spoonful of the salsa. Garnish with the additional cilantro. Any leftover salsa is great served over grilled salmon.

MAKES ABOUT 30 TO 35 PIECES

CALF LIVER

No wait—don't turn the page! You may be turned off by the thought of eating organ meats, but calf liver definitely earns its spot on the list of Paleo superfoods, especially for athletes. And with a few shopping tips and a totally doable recipe, perhaps you'll be convinced to give it a try.

Traditional cultures have long enjoyed calf liver because it is incredibly nutrient-dense, delivering a punch that few other foods can match. First, a 3-ounce (84 g) serving provides an impressive 23 grams of protein that serves as high-quality fuel for an active Paleo lifestyle. Then, there's the incredible list of vitamins and minerals it contains, including high amounts of vitamin A and several B vitamins (riboflavin, niacin, pantothenic acid, B_6, folate, and B_{12}), vitamin D, copper, iron, magnesium, phosphorus, potassium, selenium, and zinc. Calf liver covers so many nutritional bases that it acts like a natural multivitamin.

While many of the protein superfoods in this book offer these nutrients, calf liver is noteworthy because it contains them in such a high concentration, including a few that are difficult to get through dietary sources, such as the fat-soluble vitamins A and D. For example, a 3-ounce (84 g) serving of liver contains an astonishing 22,175 IU of pre-formed vitamin A—more than almost any other food, and 444 percent as much as you need daily. Your body needs vitamin A to maintain a healthy immune system and good vision, and for reproduction. Vitamin A also helps your body use the iron it has stored away, and a deficiency can lead to anemia.

Vitamin D strengthens bones by helping your body absorb calcium; it also keeps your muscles strong and allows your brain to communicate with your body. Your immune system uses vitamin D to fight off harmful bacteria and viruses as well. Calf liver offers 42 IU of vitamin D per serving, or 7 percent of what you need every day, making it a good dietary source of this hard-to-get nutrient.

Calf liver also boasts highly absorbable forms of the nutrients it contains, especially iron and B_{12}. Animal foods contain a form of iron called heme iron that your body is able to use much more effectively than the iron in plant foods (called non-heme iron). And calf liver is an excellent source, offering 5.2 milligrams per 3-ounce (84 g) serving, or nearly 30 percent of your daily requirement. Iron helps transport energizing oxygen in your blood and regulates cell growth and differentiation. Iron is especially important for people who exercise regularly and intensely—like many Paleo followers—possibly because they have a greater turnover of red blood cells. In fact, they may need up to 30 percent more iron than the recommended 18 milligrams, according to the Institute of Medicine. Liver is a great way to help you reach that goal.

Vitamin B$_{12}$ occurs naturally only in animal foods, and calf liver offers a remarkable 70.7 micrograms, or 1,178 percent of your recommended daily allowance. This B vitamin helps keep your nerve and red blood cells healthy and to form DNA, your cells' genetic material. Without enough B$_{12}$, you can experience fatigue, weakness, numbness and tingling in your hands and feet, and difficulty maintaining balance, making it hard to be active.

A FEW CAVEATS

Without a doubt, calf liver is a true Paleo superfood. However, there are a few reasons you should limit your consumption. While calf liver is one of the world's best sources of vitamin A, this critical nutrient is fat-soluble. That means your body can store up what it needs, and accumulating too much can be toxic. For this reason, you shouldn't eat liver more than once a week (and women who are pregnant or thinking about becoming pregnant shouldn't eat it at all).

Calf liver also contains 412 milligrams of cholesterol—well above the 300-milligram daily limit recommended by the American Heart Association—and 2 grams of saturated fat per 3-ounce (84 g) serving. The cholesterol content isn't too much of a concern if you have normal cholesterol levels (see "Eggs", page 20, for more on dietary cholesterol and health). But you should limit your saturated fat intake to less than 7 percent of total daily calories, or 15 grams for a 2,000 calorie-per-day diet, to avoid raising your risk of cardiovascular disease. Two grams is a small step toward that total, but it's worth noting.

SHOPPING TIPS

For the mildest flavor, look for calf liver (not beef liver) with a pale color. Calf liver is also more tender than beef liver—just be careful not to overcook it or it will become tough. As with the other Paleo protein superfoods, it's best to choose meat from animals closest to their natural state. In the case of calf liver, that means cattle that are organic, pasture-raised, and grass-fed and finished.

THE TRUTH ABOUT TOXINS

The liver does an incredible job of filtering out a daily onslaught of toxins from the body—human and bovine alike. As such, you might be concerned about eating this organ meat, for fear that those toxins accumulate and get passed on to you when you eat liver. A handful of studies, including a 2004 study published in the *International Journal of Agriculture and Biology*, have found that while beef liver does store some toxins (particularly heavy metals such as lead, cadmium, mercury, and arsenic), it does so at approximately the same concentration as the animals' lean muscle tissue. Purchasing meat from organic, pasture-raised, grass-fed and finished cattle will ensure that you get the lowest possible amounts of these and other toxins in any part of the animal.

LIVER AND BACON MEATBALLS

Organ meats are some of the most nutrient-dense foods on the planet. Unfortunately, most of us consider them the foods we are least likely to eat. I have tried every trick in the book to get my kids to eat liver, and this recipe did it.

¼ pound (112 g) grass-fed calf liver

1 pound (454 g) grass-fed beef

5 slices pastured nitrate-free bacon, cooked and diced

1½ teaspoons coconut oil

½ small sweet potato, finely diced

2 or 3 scallions, thinly sliced

1 clove garlic, minced

1 egg

½ teaspoon paprika

½ teaspoon sea salt

¼ teaspoon freshly ground black pepper

1 tablespoon (2 g) fresh parsley, minced

¼ cup (65 g) tomato paste

Preheat the oven to 375°F (190°C, or gas mark 5). Oil a baking sheet with coconut oil, or you can use nonstick aluminum foil or parchment paper to avoid a mess.

In the bowl of a food processor, process the liver until it is ground up. Add the liver to a bowl along with beef and diced cooked bacon and use your hands to mix together.

In a skillet over medium-high heat, melt the coconut oil and sauté the sweet potato until tender and golden, about 3 to 5 minutes. Add the scallions and garlic; stir and cook for an additional 30 seconds to 1 minute, until the scallions are slightly wilted and the garlic is fragrant.

Add the sweet potato mixture to the bowl with the meat mixture along with the egg, paprika, sea salt, pepper, parsley, and tomato paste, mixing with your fingers to combine. Using a scoop or a large spoon, scoop evenly sized meatballs onto the prepared baking sheet. Bake for 15 to 20 minutes, or until the meatballs are cooked through.

MAKES 15 TO 18 MEATBALLS

BONE BROTH

Bone broth, or stock, is a flavorful liquid made by boiling animal bones (typically poultry, beef, bison, lamb, or fish) in water for hours. Many people add vegetables and herbs for extra flavor. After simmering, you strain the bones and vegetables, leaving behind a delicious broth packed with vitamins, antioxidants, and minerals (especially calcium, magnesium, and phosphorous, minerals essential for bone health—and critical for dairy-free Paleo followers). Frequently used as the basis for rich-tasting soups and sauces, it's also wonderful sipped straight from a mug.

Traditional cultures worldwide have relied on bone broth as a healing food for thousands of years, and it's an easy way to get some remarkable nutrients. For example, it's a good source of gelatin and amino acids, found in connective tissue, tendons, and ligaments. Gelatin is a protein derived from collagen, a key component of cartilage and bone. Some evidence indicates that gelatin can improve osteoarthritis and boost bone and joint strength, as well as make your hair, skin, and fingernails healthier. Gelatin also contains the amino acid glycine (more on that below), which your liver needs to detoxify your body from the daily assault of environmental toxins endemic to modern life.

GLYCINE AND PROLINE

Bone broths provide good amounts of two amino acids—glycine and proline—that are key components of collagen, the most prevalent protein in the body. Collagen provides structure, strength, and flexibility to most of your body's tissues, including skin, muscle, connective tissue, and bone. Your body can make glycine and proline itself, and they play a vital role in many aspects of health.

Glycine is a critical building block not only for proteins but also for components of DNA and RNA (your genetic material) and for the oxygen-carrying hemoglobin in your red blood cells. Because glycine helps transmit chemicals in the brain, researchers are investigating whether it might be useful for improving memory and even schizophrenia. Glycine also calms inflammation in several ways, helping you heal from infection and making it a potential treatment for inflammatory diseases, note researchers from the University of North Carolina at Chapel Hill. Glycine might also help reduce the sleepiness and fatigue you feel after the occasional sleepless night, suggests a 2012 study in *Frontiers in Neurology*. And according to a 2007 study in the *Journal of Gastroenterology and Hepatology*, early evidence indicates it might even help prevent and treat cancer by inhibiting tumor growth.

Along with glycine, proline works to keep your skin healthy by building, protecting, and repairing collagen and forming new skin cells. That means that making bone broth a regular part of your diet can help heal wounds and even keep your skin more elastic, less wrinkled, and younger looking.

There's some evidence that proline, together with vitamin C and another amino acid called lysine, can also help prevent and reverse cardiovascular disease. By helping to form collagen in your artery walls, proline keeps those blood vessels flexible and healthy. It also keeps sticky fat molecules called lipoprotein(a) from forming plaques in your arteries, where they could break off and cause blockages.

BONE BROTH

Bone broth can be enjoyed by the mug-full seasoned with salt, pepper, and crushed garlic (which boosts your immune system, making this a great option for cold and flu season). It can also be used to braise meats and vegetables or as a base for soups, stews, and sauces. You can adapt this recipe to make stock from all kinds of animal bones.

Preheat the oven to 400°F (200°C, or gas mark 6).

Rinse and clean the bones under running water. Pat them dry. Place on a roasting pan and roast for about an hour, or until the bones are well browned and fragrant. (Roasting the bones ensures a good flavor in the resulting beef stock—without this step, the broth may taste sour or "off.") Once the bones are browned, drain off any fat.

Add the carrots, celery, onion, garlic, parsley, cider vinegar, and bay leaves to the pot of a slow cooker and top with the bones. Add water to cover. Cover with the lid and cook on low for 8 to 10 hours.

When the stock is finished, filter through a fine-mesh sieve and pour into a glass mason jars. Allow the stock to come to room temperature before transferring to the refrigerator. The stock should set just like gelatin, and the fat should rise to the top. Skim off the fat and reserve it for cooking, then scoop out the gelled stock and reheat to use.

The stock will keep in an airtight container in the refrigerator for up to 5 days. You can also freeze the stock for up to several months and reheat it at a later time.

MAKES APPROXIMATELY 8 CUPS (1880 ML), DEPENDING ON HOW MUCH WATER YOU USE AND HOW MUCH YOU REDUCE THE BROTH TO INTENSIFY THE FLAVOR

Note: Serve this stock very hot because it may gel again once it cools.

3 to 4 pounds (1362 to 1816 g) grass-fed beef bones

2 medium carrots, chopped

2 celery stalks, chopped

1 medium yellow onion, chopped

5 cloves garlic, smashed

4 sprigs parsley

2 tablespoons (30 ml) apple cider vinegar

2 or 3 bay leaves

BUILD A BETTER BROTH

Here's how to get the most out of any bone broth.

- Roasting beef and lamb bones first will give your broth a better color and flavor.

- Before making your broth, soak the bones in enough water to cover them, and a little vinegar for an hour or two to help extract calcium from the bones.

- To increase the amount of gelatin in your bone broth, allow the broth to cool in the refrigerator before straining.

2
PALEO SUPER GREENS

Spinach, kale, broccoli. Wait a minute, you might be thinking to yourself, these vegetables are on practically every superfood list. Doesn't everyone tell us to eat green vegetables? Well, yes, and for good reason. Greens are some of the most nutritious foods on the planet, and even though the original hunter-gatherer societies couldn't tell you about antioxidants and phyto-chemicals and all the reasons we now know *why* these foods are so good for you, they certainly knew enough to include them regularly in their diets.

But more than just being generally healthful, greens are essential to a Paleo diet for several reasons. First, because you're no longer eating dairy, you need a calcium source. These Paleo super greens—especially the dark leafy ones—provide a significant amount of calcium, plus a host of other vitamins and minerals that help build and strengthen bones. In fact, your body can absorb more calcium from most greens (40 to 64 percent) than it can from dairy products (34 percent), notes a 2009 study in the *American Journal of Clinical Nutrition*.

Second, green vegetables are absolutely packed with antioxidant phytochemicals—naturally occurring plant substances with fancy names like flavonoids and polyphenols—that protect you against an onslaught of environmental toxins and stressors that are an inescapable part of life in the twenty-first century. By defending your cells against DNA damage from oxygen-scavenging free radicals, these powerful antioxidants reduce your risk of many modern health problems, including cardiovascular disease, chronic inflammation, and cancer.

Finally, these greens provide generous amounts of fiber, which Paleo followers no longer get from grains and legumes. Fiber helps clear cholesterol from your bloodstream and speeds digestion so that waste products don't linger too long in your body (being active, like our ancestors were, helps with this, too). Certain kinds of fiber also encourage the growth of good bacteria, or probiotics, in your gut, which can improve digestive health, boost your immune system, and restore a healthy balance of bacteria after a course of antibiotics.

This chapter focuses on the best green vegetables for you to make a part of your Paleo lifestyle. And if you or someone in your household is a picky eater, the delicious recipes might just convince you to give another chance to a green you've disliked in the past (Brussels sprouts, anyone?).

SPINACH

Spinach may be the quintessential Paleo superfood. Packed with nutrients, this delicate leafy green needs to be in your regular dietary rotation. Growing up, I was often told that Popeye made himself super-strong by eating spinach. And while it's true that spinach will help you develop strong muscles, it also protects against harmful inflammation, age-accelerating free radicals, cardiovascular problems, and cancer, and strengthens your bones at the same time. It seems like my mom was right after all—good thing I believed her and ate my spinach! Here are some compelling reasons why you should eat spinach too.

Delicious, inexpensive, and versatile, spinach is a powerhouse of nutrients. Three cups of raw spinach (enough to make a decent salad, and more or less equivalent to ½ cup [90 g] cooked spinach) contains just 21 calories, but an impressive 435 micrograms of vitamin K, which is 3.6 times the amount men need daily and 4.8 times the daily requirement for women. Vitamin K allows your blood to clot and helps your body use calcium to build bones, and it might be especially important for athletes, noted a study in the *International Journal of Sports Medicine*. The researchers found that elite female athletes who supplemented with vitamin K had improved markers of bone formation.

Spinach is also a good source of vitamin A in the form of beta-carotene—3 cups (90 g) of raw spinach provides about 15 percent of what men need in a day and 20 percent of what women should get. Beta-carotene is possibly the best-known member of the family of carotenoids, antioxidant plant pigments that protect against free radicals and calm inflammation. Your body converts beta-carotene into vitamin A, which then protects your eyes, boosts immunity, and

supports your reproductive system. Vitamin A also helps cells grow and communicate properly.

Spinach provides another superstar antioxidant called lutein that also benefits your eyes by protecting against or slowing age-related macular degeneration, a leading cause of vision loss. Lutein is fat-soluble, which means you should eat spinach with a little bit of fat to increase lutein absorption.

Spinach serves up good amounts of bone-building calcium and energizing iron too, but here's where things get a little complicated. Besides all of these vitamins, minerals, and antioxidants, spinach contains an anti-nutrient called oxalic acid, or oxalate. This naturally occurring substance blocks the absorption of calcium, and spinach has a lot of it. That means your body absorbs almost none of the calcium from raw spinach, and only about 5 percent from cooked spinach (cooking spinach neutralizes some of the oxalic acid—see To Cook or Not to Cook, opposite). Oxalic acid also blocks your body's absorption of iron, although you can combat that somewhat by including a little vitamin C when you eat spinach. (Vitamin C helps convert the iron in plant foods, called non-heme iron, into the more bioavailable heme iron.)

If that weren't enough, a ½ cup (90 g) serving of cooked spinach provides 131 micrograms of folate (one-third of the recommended daily intake)—more than almost any other food except beef liver. Folate is widely recognized as an important nutrient for pregnant and nursing women, but it does more than prevent birth defects. Low levels of this B vitamin are linked to elevated levels of homocysteine, a marker of inflammation that indicates increased risk for cardiovascular disease. And population studies show that getting enough folate might protect you from several different kinds of cancer, possibly by helping to regulate cell division and the formation of DNA. Folate also helps your body metabolize amino acids, the building blocks of protein that you need for energy and to build and strengthen muscle. Looks like Popeye was on to something after all!

SHOPPING FOR SPINACH

Spinach is available in stores year-round, but you're more likely to find it at a farmers' market in spring and fall, when it is in season. Look for dark green leaves and stems with no signs of yellowing. You should buy organic spinach whenever possible—spinach occupies a place on the Environmental Working Group's Dirty Dozen. Plus, a list of the conventionally grown fruits and vegetables contaminated with the highest levels of pesticide residue. If you purchase spinach at a farmers' market or another local purveyor and the greens aren't labeled organic, ask how the spinach was grown. Many small farms forego the expensive and difficult process of having their crops certified organic, but they may still follow organic farming practices.

Spinach is also easy to grow yourself, in a garden or a container. All you need are seeds, soil, and a sunny spot. Seeds will germinate in just six to ten days, and you can start harvesting baby spinach leaves within a few weeks, or wait a few weeks longer if you'd like to harvest a whole head.

TO COOK OR NOT TO COOK?

The heat and moisture involved in cooking affect some of spinach's nutrients—for better and for worse. Cooked spinach supplies more antioxidants, such as beta-carotene and lutein, particularly if it's boiled or steamed, according to a 2008 report in the *Journal of Agriculture and Food Chemistry*. Cooking also neutralizes oxalic acid, or oxalate, the compound that prevents your body from absorbing the calcium and iron in spinach. However, heat can destroy both vitamin C and folate (although cooking method does matter—steaming seems to preserve these nutrients better than boiling, because these water-soluble nutrients leach into cooking water).

Bottom line? Do your body a favor and eat plenty of both fresh and cooked spinach (preferably with a little vitamin C and healthy fat to increase nutrient absorption) as often as you can.

SPINACH BASIL WALNUT PESTO

The vitamin K in spinach can decrease the kind of inflammation associated with osteoporosis and heart disease, according to researchers at Tufts University—all the more reason why you should include this powerhouse green in your Paleo diet.

2 cups (60 g) baby spinach

1 cup (40 g) fresh basil

1 clove garlic, sliced

¼ cup (38 g) walnuts, lightly toasted

¼ cup (60 ml) olive oil

Juice and zest of 1 lemon

Sea salt and freshly ground black pepper to taste

In the bowl of a food processor, combine all the ingredients. Process, stopping a few times to scrape down the sides of the bowl. Taste and adjust the seasoning, adding more salt, pepper, or olive oil as necessary.

MAKES 1 CUP (260 G)

TIDBIT:

Pesto can quickly add a different dimension to a dish with its amazing flavors. Have fun with this pesto by changing up the herb or even swapping the spinach for another leafy green. Bottom line: greens + herbs + nuts + garlic + olive oil = awesome!

Spinch Basil
Walnut Pesto

KALE

Kale has gotten a lot of press lately, and for good reason. This leafy green is one of the most nutrient-dense foods in existence, offering an incredible variety of vitamins, minerals, antioxidants, and other phytochemicals—beneficial substances naturally found in plants—for just a few calories per serving. A member of the cruciferous, or *Brassica*, vegetable family (along with cabbage and broccoli), kale is delicious raw in salads, tossed into soups and stews, cooked in stir-fries, added to casseroles, sautéed or braised, and even baked as crunchy kale chips (see sidebar for a bonus recipe).

A SURPRISING SOURCE OF CALCIUM

Although kale is widely considered a nutritional rock star, it earns its Paleo superfood status because of its calcium content. If you're concerned about getting enough calcium now that you've cut out dairy, make kale a mainstay in your diet. One cup (67 g) of raw chopped kale provides 100 milligrams of calcium, and unlike spinach, kale contains very low amounts of the anti-nutrient oxalic acid, which interferes with calcium absorption. In fact, your body can actually absorb the calcium in kale better than it can the calcium in dairy products, according to a study in the *American Journal of Clinical Nutrition*. Per cup, kale also contains 472 micrograms of vitamin K—more than five times what women need daily and nearly four times as much as men need—which helps your body use that calcium to strengthen and build bone.

THE ANTICANCER KING

Kale contains a slew of compounds with funny-sounding names, including sulforaphane, indole, carotenoids, kaempferol, and quercetin, that all help prevent and fight cancer. A few, including sulforaphane and indole, show a remarkable ability to target cancer cells specifically, stop them from multiplying, and even cause them to die. And indole might be especially effective against hormone-dependent cancers (including breast, cervical, and prostate cancer), according to a 2005 study in the journal *Cell Cycle*.

Some of kale's cancer-fighting compounds, such as sulforaphane, are more potent when you eat kale raw; others, such as the carotenoids beta-carotene, lutein, and zeaxanthin, are more powerful when exposed to heat. So any way you serve it, kale is a great choice.

THE CHOLESTEROL CLEANER

With 2.5 grams of fiber per ½ cup (65 g) cooked, kale is a delicious contribution to the amount of fiber (38 grams for men and 25 grams for women) that the Institute of Medicine recommends you consume every day. The fiber in kale binds to bile acids in your digestive tract, which helps lower your blood cholesterol levels and, as a result, your risk of heart disease. While raw kale provides some cholesterol-lowering benefit, steam-cooked kale is significantly better at binding those bile acids, notes a 2008 study in the journal *Nutrition Research*.

SHOPPING FOR KALE

A cool-weather vegetable, kale is abundant and slightly sweeter during mid-winter to early spring, although it's available year-round. There are several varieties of kale, including curly, ornamental, or Tuscan (also called Lacinato, black, or dinosaur kale). Nutritionally, they're pretty much equivalent, but each variety has a distinct flavor and texture.

Curly kale, not surprisingly, has ruffled leaves, plus a thick fibrous stalk. It is usually a deep green color and is the most intensely flavored of the three varieties. Ornamental kale is sometimes called salad savoy, and it's often more mellow and tender than curly kale. Its leaves can be green, white, or purple, and it's often grown to add visual interest to gardens. Tuscan kale has dark blue-green leaves with a distinctive pebbled texture. The most tender of the kale varieties, it works especially well raw in salads.

When you buy kale, look for crisp, tender, vibrantly colored leaves (avoid wilted or yellow leaves). Smaller leaves have a milder flavor and more tender texture. You can store unwashed kale in a plastic bag in the refrigerator for up to five days, but the flavor gets stronger and more bitter the longer you store it. You should also opt for organic kale whenever possible: The Environmental Working Group included kale on its 2012 Dirty Dozen Plus list because it's frequently contaminated with organophosphate insecticides, which are highly toxic to the nervous system.

BONUS RECIPE

KALE CHIPS

Kale chips are incredibly easy to make, and they're a much healthier alternative to potato chips or other processed snacks. Some people think curly kale makes the best kale chips, but feel free to experiment with Tuscan kale as well, and to add your favorite spices. To make the chips, preheat your oven to 375°F (190°C, or gas mark 5). Rinse one bunch of kale leaves well and pat them dry thoroughly. Cut out the thick stalks and roughly chop the leaves. Toss with 1 tablespoon (15 ml) olive oil or coconut oil, 1 minced clove of garlic, and a sprinkle of salt and pepper. Spread out on a large rimmed baking sheet and bake for about 15 minutes, stirring a few times, until the leaves are crisp but still tender.

MAKES ABOUT 4 CUPS (136 G)

SLOW COOKER CHICKEN, SWEET POTATO, AND KALE STEW

Kale packs this stew with a wealth of vitamins and minerals. Change it up and add a combo of other leafy greens, such as Swiss chard and spinach. Just be sure to remove the thickest center ribs before breaking leaves into pieces and wash well to remove any grittiness.

1 pound (454 g) skinless, boneless, pasture-raised chicken breasts

1 yellow onion, diced

3 carrots, peeled and cubed

1 large sweet potato, peeled and cubed

3 cloves garlic, minced

1 cup (235 ml) low-sodium chicken broth

⅓ cup (90 g) tomato paste

3 tablespoons (45 ml) balsamic vinegar

2 teaspoons gluten-free yellow mustard

3 bay leaves

1 bunch kale, stems removed and broken into pieces

Sea salt and freshly ground black pepper to taste

Wash the chicken and cut into bite-size pieces. Place into the pot of a slow cooker.

On top of the chicken add the diced onion, cubed carrots, cubed sweet potato, garlic, chicken broth, tomato paste, balsamic vinegar, mustard, and bay leaves. Stir to mix everything together. Turn the slow cooker on high heat for 3 to 4 hours, or until the carrots and sweet potato are tender. Add the kale and stir to combine; cook for 1 hour more.

Taste the stew and season with sea salt and pepper. Remove the bay leaves and serve.

MAKES 5 TO 6 SERVINGS

TIP:

If you don't like your chicken chunky, you can add the chicken breasts whole and shred the chicken at the end of cooking by using a fork or the back of a spoon. Using the slow cooker to cook the chicken makes this super easy to do. I've had the stew both ways, and both are delicious.

BRUSSELS SPROUTS

Ahhh, Brussels sprouts! Many people have a love-'em or hate-'em relationship with these green veggies, especially if you were raised eating them reheated from frozen or boiled into oblivion. But even if you've shied away from sprouts in the past, this Paleo super-food is worth a second look. I grew up in a Brussels sprout–free home and only just found in the last few years how delicious fresh sprouts are. Try them lightly steamed or sautéed (their pleasantly bitter flavor pairs well with the salty bite of bacon, or with tangy mustard), as an unexpected addition to stir-fries, or even shredded raw as a salad or added to frittatas or quiches. Oven-roasting sprouts brings out their nutty sweetness.

They look like miniature cabbages, but don't be fooled by their small size—Brussels sprouts are little nutritional powerhouses. One cup (88 g) of raw Brussels sprouts boasts 3 grams of muscle-building protein to help you get lean and strong, and 3 grams of cholesterol-clearing fiber, helping make up for the lack of fiber-rich grains and legumes in the Paleo diet. Sprouts are also a good source of potassium (essential for healthy muscle function) and vitamin K (which helps blood clot and strengthens bones). Like their cruciferous cousins, including kale, broccoli, and cabbage, Brussels sprouts are rich in nutrients that fight cancer, keep your cardiovascular system healthy, boost your immune system, and help calm inflammation.

SULFUR-CONTAINING COMPOUNDS

Brussels sprouts contain a group of phytonutrients (beneficial plant compounds) called glucosinolates that give cooked sprouts their distinct smell. Your body converts these sulfur-containing compounds into isothiocyanates that are responsible for many of Brussels sprouts' health benefits, including protecting you from cancer, aiding the liver in detoxification, and calming harmful inflammation throughout your body—some of the main goals of the Paleo diet. Heat lowers the concentration of glucosinolates and isothiocyanates, notes a 2011 study in the *Journal of Food Science*, so be careful not to overcook Brussels sprouts (this will also minimize any unpleasant odor).

One isothiocyanate called sulforaphane appears to be especially effective at calming inflammation, thereby reducing your risk of cardiovascular disease. Inflammation can trigger plaque buildup in your arteries, making them stiff and blocking blood flow. But sulforaphane signals genes in your cells to fight back against that damage and keep your blood vessels healthy. A 2011 study in *The EPMA Journal* found that sulforaphane suppressed inflammation in the branches and bends of arteries—locations that are more susceptible to atherosclerosis.

ANTIOXIDANTS

By weight, Brussels sprouts contain about 50 percent more vitamin C than an orange. Antioxidant vitamin C fights free radicals to help keep skin healthy and strengthen your immune system.

Vitamins E and A (in the form of beta-carotene) do their part to mop up free radicals and prevent oxidative damage to your cells as well. The antioxidants in Brussels sprouts also defend your DNA against free radical damage, which appears to be one of the ways they help protect you from developing cancer, according to a 2008 study in *Molecular Nutrition and Food Research*.

Brussels sprouts are an excellent source—possibly the best of the cruciferous veggies—of a group of antioxidants known as flavonoids. Flavonoids belong to a larger class of plant antioxidants called polyphenols, and a French study that compared the polyphenol content of fruits and vegetables listed Brussels sprouts as having 2.6 times more total polyphenols than broccoli and 20.5 times more than cauliflower.

BRUSSELS SPROUT BASICS

When you shop for Brussels sprouts, look for bright green, firm, compact heads with tightly packed leaves. (But watch out for leaves with holes in them—that's a sign that insects might be living inside.) They're sold still attached to the stalk or, more commonly, loose, and you'll be able to find them more readily in the cool weather months when they're in season (September to mid-February). You can keep unwashed sprouts in the refrigerator for 10 to 14 days.

When you're ready to use the Brussels sprouts, trim the stems and remove any yellow or discolored leaves. Wash them well under running water and shake or pat dry. Cut them in half or into quarters to cook them, or shred sprouts if using them raw.

FUN FACTS

THE NAME GAME: Brussels sprouts get their name because they were cultivated in Brussels, Belgium, 800 years ago.

MIGRATION OF MINIATURE CABBAGES: In the United States, French settlers first brought Brussels sprouts to Louisiana, but today most of the country's sprouts are grown in the central coast of California, where the cool temperatures and fog provide ideal growing conditions. The rest are grown in New York State.

A LOVE-HATE RELATIONSHIP: A 2005 poll named Brussels sprouts as Britain's fifth favorite vegetable, but in a 2013 survey commissioned by the National Trust, 15 percent of people polled voted Brussels sprouts their least favorite vegetable. Still, the British remain the world's top Brussels sprout consumers, growing six to seven times as many crops as the United States.

ROASTED FALL VEGETABLES

When fall weather arrives and the leaves start to change outside, there is nothing better than a plate of seasonal roasted vegetables. In this dish, the sweetness from the fruit and squash makes a nice counterpoint to the slight bitterness of the sprouts' super-healthy sulfur-containing compounds.

1 pound (454 g) Brussels sprouts

1 small sweet potato, peeled and cut into ½-inch (1.3 cm) cubes

1 Fuji apple, cut into ½-inch (1.3 cm) cubes

1 pear, cut into ½-inch (1.3 cm) cubes

¼ butternut squash, peeled and cut into ½-inch (1.3 cm) cubes

½ teaspoon sea salt

½ teaspoon ground cinnamon

2½ tablespoons (35 g) coconut oil, melted

⅓ cup (50 g) toasted pecans, chopped

Preheat the oven to 425°F (220°C, or gas mark 7) and line a baking sheet with foil or parchment paper.

Wash the Brussels sprouts and cut the ends off, then cut into halves or quarters depending on how big your sprouts are. (The goal is to try to have all the fruit and veggies in this dish about the same size so they cook evenly.)

Combine the Brussels sprouts, sweet potato cubes, apple cubes, pear cubes, butternut squash cubes, sea salt, and cinnamon in a large bowl and toss together. Drizzle the melted coconut oil over the mixture and toss to coat evenly. Pour onto the prepared baking sheet and spread into a single layer.

Roast for 20 to 30 minutes, or until the veggies and fruit are soft and tender. The cooking time will depend on how large you make your cubes, too. Right after removing the pan from the oven, sprinkle the toasted chopped pecans over the top and stir to combine. Serve immediately.

MAKES 4 OR 5 SERVINGS

COLLARD GREENS

When I was growing up in the southern United States, it was common to find collard greens on the dinner table. I distinctly remember the smell of my grandmother's kitchen when collards were on the stove. Little did I know that these greens were a Paleo superfood chock-full of essential nutrients. With their very mild, almost smoky flavor, collards stand out as a delicious way to boost your health.

Like other vegetables in the cruciferous family, it's important not to overcook collards. Not only does overcooking them increase their smell (the longer they cook, the more sulfur-containing compounds they release), but it can also reduce the health benefits of those compounds. A quick five-minute steam, sauté, or stir-fry is all you need to render collard greens tender and tasty.

ATHLETES' CHOICE

If you exercise regularly, like many Paleo followers do, collard greens are great fuel for your workouts. One cup (130 g) of cooked collards provides 5 grams of protein to give you long-lasting energy and repair the microscopic tears in muscle fiber that occur when you exercise. Collards also offer 2 grams of iron to carry energizing oxygen through your blood, helping you work out longer and harder. And collards' substantial vitamin A content, in the form of antioxidant beta-carotene, improves lung function, helping you breathe easier as you exercise. In fact, it might even help treat respiratory infections, notes a 2003 study in the journal *Molecular Aspects of Medicine*.

FIBER-TASTIC

Collard greens serve up an impressive 7 grams of fiber, which aids digestion. (Note: If you're new to eating Paleo, with its emphasis on fiber-rich vegetables and fruits, be sure to drink plenty of water every day to help your digestive system adjust.) Fiber also binds to bile acids and cholesterol in your digestive tract, which prevents you from absorbing them. Your body compensates by pulling LDL ("bad") cholesterol from your bloodstream to use instead, thereby lowering your blood cholesterol levels and reducing your risk of heart disease. Steam cooking increases this cholesterol-lowering effect, according to a 2008 study in the journal *Nutrition Research*, but remember not to overcook your collards. Additionally, fiber can help keep your blood sugar steady so it doesn't spike and send you in search of refined carbs for a quick pick-me-up.

BONE BOOSTER

When you're not eating dairy, consuming enough calcium can be tricky. Enter collard greens! Like its cousins spinach and kale, collards provide a considerable amount of calcium—268 milligrams per cup (130 g) of cooked greens. While collards do contain some of the anti-nutrient oxalic acid, which partly prevents your body from absorbing calcium (and iron), cooking helps neutralize it so it's less of an issue. Collard greens also offer a stellar 772 micrograms of vitamin K to help your body absorb and use that calcium. That's so much vitamin K—nearly six and a half times as much as men need and eight and a half times as much as women need daily—that you might actually need to limit your consumption if you take a blood-thinning medication or have any kind of bleeding problems! Collards contribute several other minerals critical for bone health as well, including potassium (222 milligrams), magnesium (41 milligrams), and phosphorus (61 milligrams).

COOKING COLLARDS

Collard greens have broad, smooth leaves with edible stalks, and they are in season from November through April. When shopping for collards, keep in mind that smaller leaves are more tender and have a milder flavor. Choose bunches that have firm leaves and show no signs of yellowing or browning. Like kale, collard greens occupy a spot on the 2012 Environmental Working Group's Dirty Dozen Plus list because they are often contaminated with highly toxic organophosphate pesticides. Buy organic whenever possible (or check with your farmer or market to make sure they don't use these pesticides).

Collard greens will keep in the refrigerator for up to one week. Before cooking your collards, rinse them well to remove any dirt and grit. Then chop the leaves into ½-inch (1.3 cm) slices and the stems into ¼-inch (6 mm) pieces for quick and even cooking.

OMEGA-3S IN COLLARD GREENS?

That's right, 1 cup (130 g) of cooked collards (and other dark leafy greens such as spinach, kale, and dandelion greens) provides 0.2 gram of omega-3s in the form of alpha-linolenic acid (ALA). Your body converts ALA into the fatty acids eicosapentaenoic acid (EPA) and docosahexaenoic acid (DHA), the two omega-3s most studied for their health benefits. EPA and DHA keep your cardiovascular system healthy and calm harmful inflammation, and DHA is particularly important for brain development and function. While collard greens aren't a stellar source of omega-3s—nowhere near salmon's 1.7 grams per 4-ounce (112 g) portion, for example—they can help you reach the 0.8 to 1.1 grams of alpha-linolenic acid that the World Health Organization recommends consuming each day.

COLLARD WRAPS WITH SPICED AIOLI DIPPING SAUCE

These wraps make a perfect lunch or light dinner, and if the only greens you tend to eat are spinach and romaine lettuce, collards are a fantastic way to diversify, both in flavor and nutritional profile. Be sure to include the spiced dipping sauce to give these wraps an extra kick.

FOR WRAPS:

4 large collard leaves

2 pastured-raised organic chicken breasts, grilled and cut into strips

½ raw zucchini, cut into small strips

1 carrot, shredded

6 large strawberries, thinly sliced

1 medium avocado, sliced

⅓ cup (13 g) fresh basil, chopped

FOR SPICED AIOLI DIPPING SAUCE:

⅓ cup (75 g) homemade mayonnaise (page 178)

1½ teaspoons fresh chives, chopped

½ teaspoon garlic powder

¼ teaspoon chili powder

Juice from ½ lime

Sea salt to taste

To make the wraps: Wash the collard greens and use a knife to carefully cut out any big stems. Don't cut the leaves in half—only remove as much as you need to get the thick parts out. Then steam the collard leaves for 1 to 2 minutes, or just until tender.

Divide the remaining wrap ingredients except the basil evenly among the collard leaves. Sprinkle the chopped basil over everything. Fold the bottom edge of the collard leaf over the filling, followed by the sides, then roll as tightly as you can—still being gentle—until you get to the end of the leaf. Hold in place with a toothpick and cut in half on a slight angle.

To make the dipping sauce: Place all the ingredients in the bowl of a food processor and process until smooth.

Serve the wraps with the spiced aioli sauce for dipping.

MAKES 4 WRAPS

ASPARAGUS

After a long winter, asparagus is one of the first signs of spring. Delicious raw, it's an unexpected addition to salads. But it doesn't take long to cook, either, and it's incredibly versatile—try asparagus steamed, sautéed, oven-roasted, or grilled; at room temperature, hot, or cold; and tossed into soups, casseroles, stir-fries, and egg dishes, or as a standalone side dish.

This beautiful green vegetable doesn't land on many superfood lists, but it should. A member of the lily family, asparagus is fast growing and nutrient-dense. One cup (120 g) of asparagus (about 10 small spears) provides 2.8 grams of fiber; nearly 3 grams of iron; 271 milligrams of potassium; vitamins A, C, and E; plus good amounts of almost all the B vitamins. And with its ability to fight free radicals, help your body detoxify, and calm inflammation—key goals of the Paleo diet—asparagus is a great addition to your Paleo repertoire.

ANTIOXIDANTS

Asparagus is often overlooked as an antioxidant powerhouse, but it boasts good amounts of numerous antioxidant nutrients, including vitamin C, beta-carotene, vitamin E, and the minerals zinc, manganese, and selenium, that work to neutralize cell-damaging free radicals. And when researchers compared the anti-oxidant activities of asparagus and broccoli (widely recognized for its high antioxidant content), asparagus actually came out on top! That's likely because asparagus contains more flavonoids—naturally occurring plant pigments that function as antioxidants in our bodies—than broccoli, noted a 2007 study in the journal *Food Chemistry*.

Asparagus is also one of the best vegetable sources of glutathione, the body's most abundant free radical scavenger. Your body makes glutathione naturally from three amino acids (glutamic acid, cysteine, and glycine), but your ability to produce it declines as you get older. Eating foods such as asparagus that contain preformed glutathione can help boost your levels. Glutathione is the primary antioxidant in the brain, protecting your brain cells from free radical damage and inflammation. It also plays a crucial role in detoxifying your body of foreign chemical compounds, and helps prevent (or at least delay) cataracts from forming in your eyes as you get older. By counteracting oxidative stress, glutathione protects against premature aging and a whole host of health problems, including Alzheimer's, Parkinson's disease, cancer, cardiovascular disease, and diabetes.

BONUS RECIPE

OVEN-ROASTED ASPARAGUS

This side dish couldn't be simpler, and it's an excellent accompaniment to all kinds of meat dishes. Preheat your oven to 450°F (230°C, or gas mark 8). Trim the woody ends off of 1 pound (454 g) of asparagus stalks. Rinse well and pat dry. In a large roasting pan, toss the asparagus with 1½ teaspoons avocado oil, ghee, or Paleo oil of choice and ¼ teaspoon salt. Roast for 8 to 10 minutes, until tender and lightly browned.

MAKES 4 SERVINGS

INULIN

Asparagus contains a unique type of carbohydrate called inulin. This starchy substance doesn't break down in your stomach; instead, it passes undigested into your large intestine. There, inulin acts like a prebiotic—a natural food source for beneficial bacteria (such as *Bifidobacteria* and *Lactobacilli*, known as probiotics) that improve digestion and nutrient absorption, especially of minerals. Early research suggests that inulin may also lower the risk of allergy, colon cancer, and diabetes, notes a 2012 review in the journal *Phytotherapy Research*.

If you've been sick, and especially if you've taken antibiotics, the balance of good and bad bacteria in your gut might be off, leading to some digestive distress. And while cultured dairy, such as yogurt, replenishes good bacteria, it's not a Paleo-friendly food. So what do you do? Pile asparagus onto your plate to support the growth of good bacteria.

SHOPPING FOR ASPARAGUS

Peak asparagus season is from late March through May, although in California crops are picked as early as February, and in the Midwest and the East Coast, the harvest can go as late as July. In addition to the familiar green stalks you've seen at the market, you can find the more delicate and mellow-flavored white asparagus, which is grown underground to prevent photosynthesis from taking place, and the smaller purple asparagus, which has a slightly fruitier flavor.

Fresh, tender asparagus has firm, thin stalks with compact tips and cut ends that don't look dried out. As soon as you get your asparagus home, either wrap the cut ends in a damp paper towel or stand the stalks in ½ inch (1.3 cm) of cold water in a container and store in the refrigerator. Even with these steps, asparagus is highly perishable, so you'll want to eat it within a day or two of purchasing.

WHAT'S THAT SMELL?

It's not your imagination—your urine really does smell different after you eat asparagus, but no one is exactly sure why. Researchers have proposed some twenty-one different substances as a possible cause, but there's no conclusive evidence to say which one (or ones) is really to blame.

However, according to a 2011 study in the journal *Chemical Senses*, a small percentage of people don't seem to produce the odor and an equally small percentage of people can't smell it (at least not in concentrations found in human urine).

ASPARAGUS WITH TARRAGON VINAIGRETTE

One cup of asparagus provides 70 micrograms of the water-soluble B vitamin folate, or folic acid, which helps produce healthy red blood cells and is critically important for preventing birth defects.

1 pound (454 g) fresh asparagus, trimmed

2 cloves garlic, minced

2 tablespoons (30 ml) apple cider vinegar

1 tablespoon (4 g) fresh tarragon, chopped

1 teaspoon gluten-free Dijon mustard

6 tablespoons (90 ml) extra-virgin olive oil

Sea salt and freshly ground black pepper

Fill a large pot with water to depth of 1 inch (2.5 cm) and bring to a boil over high heat. Place the asparagus on a steamer rack set over the water. Cover the pot and steam until the asparagus is crisp and tender, about 4 minutes. Transfer the asparagus to a bowl of ice water and cool. Drain. Place the asparagus on paper towels.

Combine the garlic, vinegar, tarragon, and mustard in a bowl. Gradually whisk in the oil. Season with sea salt and pepper, to taste.

Arrange the asparagus on a serving platter and drizzle with the vinaigrette.

MAKES 4 SERVINGS

TIP:

Tarragon can add an unexpected punch to a dish. A member of the lettuce family, tarragon has tender leaves with an anise flavor. Not a fan of the anise flavor of tarragon? Try using other woody herbs such as rosemary, oregano, or thyme.

BROCCOLI

Broccoli is another one of those love-it-or-hate-it vegetables, but nutritionally, there's a lot to love. If you fall into the "hate it" camp, consider trying a different preparation—instead of boiled or frozen and reheated, which can ruin broccoli's wonderfully crisp texture, try it lightly steamed, sautéed, stir-fried, blanched, or even oven-roasted. Or if you studiously avoid the broccoli on crudité platters, try finely chopping raw spears and tossing them into salads, where they'll partly be disguised by other vegetables.

Any way you serve it, broccoli has a prominent reputation as a superfood, and it's well deserved. In addition to being a good source of fiber, calcium, iron, potassium, and an alphabet's worth of vitamins—including a full day's worth of vitamins C and K—a single cup (70 g) of chopped broccoli (or about three 5-inch [12.5 cm] spears) provides a surprising 2.5 grams of protein and 19 milligrams of anti-inflammatory omega-3s. In fact, it contains omega-3s and omega-6s in a nearly 1:1 ratio (with slightly more omega-3s), which is the ideal ratio that the Paleo diet tries to achieve. But broccoli also offers a wealth of healthful compounds you won't find listed on the nutrition facts label, and those contribute significantly to broccoli's superfood status.

ANTIMICROBIAL SUPPORT

We're going to get a little technical for a second, so hang in there. Out of all the cruciferous vegetables, broccoli supplies the highest levels of sulfur-containing compounds called glucosinolates. When you chew broccoli, an enzyme called myrosinase breaks down glucosinolates so your body can use them once they reach your digestive tract. Those breakdown products include isothiocyanates, of which sulforaphane is one (more on that later), which help protect your body against harmful bacteria. Remarkably, some glucosinolates in broccoli are as effective against *Staphylococcus* and *Salmonella* as the antibiotics typically used to treat them, according to a 2012 study in the journal *Bioorganic & Medicinal Chemistry Letters*. Cooking inactivates myrosinase, so for the most health benefits, opt for raw broccoli at least some of the time (or at least make sure it keeps some of its crunch if you do cook it—that means about 2 to 3 minutes of total cooking time).

CANCER PROTECTION

Sulforaphane, which is probably the best-known isothiocyanate, has gotten a lot of attention for its protective effects against cancer cells in lab and animal studies. In addition to helping detoxify environmental carcinogens from your normal healthy cells, sulforaphane may switch on certain genes that suppress tumor growth. It also seems to have the ability to target cancer cells, stop them from growing, and kill them, according to a 2008 review in *Cancer Letters*. Interestingly, sulforaphane supplements don't work nearly as well as actually eating broccoli. Although your gut does contain some of the enzyme myrosinase that breaks down sulforaphane's parent compound, glucosinolate, so your body can use it, research shows that the myrosinase that you release by chewing broccoli is about five times more effective.

BLOOD SUGAR BALANCE

One of the hallmarks of the Paleo diet is its ability to help prevent relatively modern diseases such as metabolic syndrome and diabetes. That's partly due to Paleo superfoods such as broccoli, which contain high levels of fiber and chromium to help stabilize blood sugar levels. Chromium is a metallic element that helps your body use glucose to meet its energy needs so it doesn't have to pump out extra insulin. But chromium gets stripped out of foods, especially sugars and flours, during the refining process. That means people who eat a lot of refined foods are at risk of chromium deficiency, and as a result, have higher odds of developing diabetes, metabolic syndrome, and other blood sugar disorders. Even a mild chromium deficiency can trigger fatigue. On the flip side, if you follow the Paleo principle of eating only real, whole foods—including Paleo superfoods such as broccoli, which is one of the best vegetable sources of chromium with 22 micrograms per cup (70 g)—you can significantly lower your risk of these diseases and ensure you have plenty of energy.

BROCCOLI—NATURE'S ALLERGY MEDICINE?

A handful of lab studies indicate that several of the flavonoids (naturally occurring plant pigments) in broccoli may help calm allergies. The flavonoids, including kaempferol and quercetin, inhibit the release of inflammatory substances such as histamine and chemical messengers called pro-inflammatory cytokines that cause allergy symptoms. Broccoli is a very good source of kaempferol in particular, and it's the major contributor of kaempferol to the diet, according to the U.S. Department of Agriculture. More research needs to be done, but if you suffer from allergies, it certainly can't hurt to eat more broccoli!

BRINGING HOME THE BROCCOLI

Broccoli's peak growing season is October through April, although you can find it in markets year-round. Look for heads with compact florets and firm stalks. Avoid yellowing heads or stalks with wilted leaves. Stored in your refrigerator's crisper drawer, unwashed broccoli should keep for seven to ten days. (Cut or chopped broccoli loses its vitamin C more quickly, so store the heads uncut or use within a few days.)

SPICY BROCCOLI AND BEEF STIR-FRY

This quick, flavor-packed dish makes life easy on busy weeknights. Broccoli is a super-nutritious choice, thanks to its free radical–fighting flavonoids, but you can swap in other vegetables to add even more flavor, nutrients, and antioxidants. I like to serve this stir-fry over cauliflower rice (see note).

1½ tablespoons (23 ml) toasted sesame oil*

3 cloves garlic, minced

1½ tablespoons (9 g) minced fresh ginger

1 pound (454 g) grass-fed beef, cut into 1-inch (2.5 cm) chunks

4 cups (280 g) broccoli florets

¼ cup (33 g) thinly sliced scallion

⅓ cup (60 ml) coconut amino sauce**

½ teaspoon red pepper flakes

Sea salt, to taste

*Sesame oil gives this dish the Asian flair it deserves. However, it is not one of the Paleo superfood fats of choice. If you prefer, you can use coconut oil instead, but you won't get the same flavor.

**See Resources, page 214.

Heat the sesame oil in a large skillet or wok over medium-high heat, add the garlic and ginger, and sauté for 1 to 2 minutes, or until fragrant. Add the beef and stir. Continue to cook the beef until browned on all sides, about 5 minutes. Add the broccoli and continue to sauté over high heat, about 2 to 3 minutes. Then add the scallion, stirring to combine. Add the coconut amino sauce and season with red pepper flakes and sea salt.

Continue to sauté for an additional 2 minutes, until all the flavors are combined and the broccoli is tender.

Serve immediately over cauliflower rice (see below), or on its own.

MAKES 4 OR 5 SERVINGS

BONUS RECIPE

CAULIFLOWER RICE

In a large skillet, heat 2 tablespoons (28 g) ghee, bacon grease, or coconut oil over medium heat. Add 1 medium diced onion and sauté for 10 minutes, or until soft. Add 1 minced garlic clove and sauté for 5 minutes.

Meanwhile, place 1 head of cauliflower in a food processor. Process until the cauliflower is the texture of rice. Add the cauliflower to the skillet, cover, and cook 5 to 10 minutes, or until soft. Season with salt and pepper to taste.

MAKES 3 CUPS (500 G)

SWISS CHARD

Aristotle wrote about chard in the fourth century BCE, so it's no surprise that even today this delicious leafy green is still a staple of Mediterranean cooking. You can use Swiss chard in almost any way that you would use spinach—raw in salads or on sandwiches; added to soups, stews, casseroles, or egg dishes; or blanched, braised, sautéed, or steamed as a side dish. Swiss chard is a stellar source of nutrients such as vitamins A, C, and K, and it provides good amounts of magnesium, potassium, iron, and fiber.

BONE BOOSTER

Like many other leafy green vegetables, Swiss chard supplies large amounts of bone-building calcium, magnesium, and vitamin K. With 102 milligrams of calcium per cup (70 g), cooked Swiss chard is an important addition to a dairy-free Paleo diet. While chard does contain a fair amount of oxalic acid, the anti-nutrient that prevents you from absorbing calcium, cooking can help reduce that effect and allow your body to get the calcium it needs.

QUICK TIP:

Don't cook Swiss chard in non-anodized aluminum pots or pans—its oxalic acid will react with the metal and cause it to discolor.

Magnesium is the fourth most abundant mineral in the body, and about half of that is found in your bones. Magnesium affects calcium metabolism and the hormones that regulate the way your body uses calcium, so even a mild deficiency can put your bones at risk. Most people eating the typical American diet don't get enough magnesium, and if you take antibiotics or diuretics to control your blood pressure, you're even more likely to be deficient. But increasing your dietary intake can boost your body's stores of magnesium and improve bone mineral density, according to a 1999 study in the *American Journal of Clinical Nutrition*. Just 1 cup (130 g) of cooked chard provides 150 milligrams (about 38 percent of your recommended daily allowance) of this critical mineral.

With a whopping 573 micrograms of vitamin K, 1 cup (130 g) of cooked Swiss chard provides nearly five times as much as men need and more than six times as much as women need on a daily basis. That's great news for your bones, which need vitamin K to use calcium. Without enough vitamin K, you're likely to have low bone mineral density and have a greater risk of fractures, notes a 2008 study in the journal *Vitamins and Hormones*.

VISION SAVER

Swiss chard offers an abundance of carotenoids, primarily red, yellow, and orange plant pigments that act as antioxidants to mop up damaging free radicals. Three of chard's carotenoids in particular—beta-carotene, lutein, and zeaxanthin—help keep your eyes healthy. Your body converts beta-carotene into vitamin A, which promotes good vision (especially at night), helps prevent annoying dry eye, and may help reduce your risk of developing cataracts and age-related macular degeneration, the leading cause of blindness in people over fifty.

BLOOD SUGAR STABILIZER

If you've "gone Paleo" to help reduce your risk of diabetes or to lose weight, Swiss chard should be one of your primary Paleo superfoods. One cup (130 g) of cooked chard provides 3.7 grams of fiber and 3.3 grams of protein, both of which help steady your blood sugar levels. Fiber and protein slow the digestive process, delivering a steady supply of energy to your cells and preventing the spike and crash that can send you into a tailspin (and craving calorie-dense carbs for a quick pick-me-up).

But Swiss chard has another blood sugar–regulating trick up its sleeve. It also contains a flavonoid called syringic acid that inhibits an enzyme that breaks down carbohydrates into simple sugars. That helps steady your blood sugar, especially after a meal, and might be helpful in treating or preventing diabetes and other blood sugar disorders, notes a 2010 study in *Mini Reviews in Medicinal Chemistry*.

DID YOU KNOW?

Although Swiss chard has been around at least since the ancient Greeks, a Swiss botanist named Koch finally gave it its scientific name (*Beta vulgaris*) in the nineteenth century. A member of the beet family, Swiss chard goes by a multitude of names, including white beet, strawberry spinach, seakale beet, leaf beet, Sicilian beet, spinach beet, Chilean beet, Roman kale, perpetual spinach, silverbeet, and mangold.

SHOPPING FOR SWISS CHARD

Grocery stores and farmers' markets generally carry three varieties of Swiss chard: rainbow (which has a colorful red, pink, yellow, or white stalk), Fordhook Giant (which has a thick, tender, white stalk and crinkly leaves), and Ruby Red (which has thin red stalks and a slightly stronger flavor). Whichever variety you choose, look for bright green, shiny leaves with no marks, holes, or blemishes, and crisp stalks. Cleaning chard can be a challenge—the nooks and crannies of the leaves hold on to dust and dirt quite well. To get rid of the grit, submerge the leaves in a bowl of cold water and swish them around. Then rinse the leaves under running water and repeat several times. To store, wrap the leaves in a damp paper towel and place them in a plastic bag in your refrigerator's crisper drawer, where they'll keep for two or three days. Both the leaves and the stalks are edible, but the lower portion of the stalk may be tough and fibrous. Feel free to cut it off if you like.

BREAKFAST HASH WITH BELL PEPPER AND SWISS CHARD

Bitter greens and rich egg are one of those perfect flavor combinations. Cooking the greens for just a few minutes reduces the nutrient-blocking effect of chard's oxalic acid but ensures they won't release too many of their smelly sulfurous compounds.

3 tablespoons (42 g) coconut oil or bacon grease, divided

½ yellow onion, diced

½ red bell pepper, seeded and diced

1 sweet potato, peeled and diced

1 bunch Swiss chard, stems removed, leaves cut crosswise into 1-inch (2.5 cm) strips

Sea salt and freshly ground black pepper to taste

4 to 6 eggs

8 to 12 slices nitrate-free pasture-raised bacon, cooked

In a large sauté pan over medium heat, warm 1 tablespoon (14 g) of the coconut oil. Add the onion and bell pepper and cook, stirring occasionally, until the onion is caramelized, about 5 to 10 minutes. Transfer to a bowl.

Increase the heat to medium-high and add 1 tablespoon (14 g) coconut oil to the pan. Add the sweet potato and cook, tossing occasionally, until lightly brown and tender, about 5 to 8 minutes. Return the onion mixture to the pan and toss to combine. Add the chard to the pan and cook, stirring occasionally, until wilted, about 3 to 4 minutes. Add sea salt and pepper to taste.

Set a large nonstick skillet over medium heat and let it warm up. Add 1 to 3 teaspoons (5 to 14 g) of the remaining coconut oil. Crack the eggs directly into the pan and let them sit. They will be done when the whites are set and the outer edges are just starting to curl up. If the edges start to curl before the whites in the center are fully cooked, cover the skillet with a lid for a minute or two.

Divide the hash evenly among plates and top each with a fried egg. Serve immediately with a side of bacon.

MAKES 4 TO 6 SERVINGS

CABBAGE

The humble cabbage belongs to the cruciferous, or Brassica, vegetable family and is related to kale, broccoli, collards, and Brussels sprouts. There are several varieties—green, savoy, Napa, red, and Chinese (or bok choy), among others—and each has different characteristics and a slightly different nutritional profile. This ancient food is popular in many ethnic cuisines and is quite versatile—you can steam, sauté, stir-fry, braise, stew, or blanch it, or shred it and serve it raw. In general, eating cabbage raw or lightly cooked best preserves its health benefits. But any way you serve it, this Paleo superfood provides an abundance of free radical–scavenging antioxidants, good amounts of vitamins C and K and blood pressure–lowering potassium, and even a little bit of muscle-building protein. Regularly including cabbage in your diet can help protect you from a host of modern-day ills, including cancer and obesity, that were virtually nonexistent when our ancestors walked the earth.

CANCER FIGHTER

Brassica vegetables, including cabbage, contain ten different kinds of glucosinolates, sulfur-containing plant chemicals that have anti-carcinogenic activity. Your body breaks down glucosinolates into compounds called isothiocyanates that help neutralize environmental carcinogens. Specific isothiocyanates, such as sulforaphane, may target cancer cells and inhibit their growth or cause them to die, according to a 2008 review in the journal Cancer Letters. Heat can destroy the enzyme that breaks down glucosinolates, so serve your cabbage raw or only lightly cooked so it keeps its crunch (less than five minutes should do the trick).

Cabbage also contains plant pigments that act as antioxidants to protect you against free radical damage that can lead to cell damage and, ultimately, cancer. Different varieties of cabbage offer different protective plant pigments—for example, red cabbage contains more of the purple anthocyanins, and savoy cabbage contains more beta-carotene and lutein than green cabbage. Incorporate all the varieties into your diet for the best antioxidant protection.

WAISTLINE TRIMMER

No, I'm not talking about the infamous (and totally unsustainable!) cabbage soup diet. But if our modern way of eating has left you carrying a few extra pounds, including cabbage regularly in your diet can help you lose weight—or stay at a healthy weight—safely. For just 22 calories, 1 cup (90 g) of chopped raw cabbage offers 2.2 grams of fiber, which helps you feel full longer, promotes healthy digestion, and helps stabilize your blood sugar and curb cravings for the refined carbs and sugars you're trying to avoid as a Paleo follower.

Red cabbage may be particularly useful in managing blood sugar, because the anthocyanins it contains can help regulate the amount of insulin you release after a meal. And the higher your anthocyanin intake, the lower your risk for type 2 diabetes, according to a 2011 study in the American Journal of Clinical Nutrition.

NAVIGATING THE CABBAGE PATCH

Available year-round, cabbage has a peak season in late fall and winter. It's inexpensive and keeps well (uncut, cabbage should keep for up to two weeks; chopped, it's good for about five or six days). Choose cabbage heads that are firm, heavy, and brightly colored, and steer clear of leaves with bruises or holes—severe damage indicates pests or decay that may go all the way to the core.

SUPER SAUERKRAUT

Archaeological evidence indicates that fermented foods have been around since 1.5 million years BCE. Fermented foods such as sauerkraut contain beneficial bacteria, known as probiotics, that can help maintain a healthy gut. An imbalance of good and bad bacteria can damage your intestinal lining and lead to digestive troubles, but it can also trigger inflammation and health problems throughout your body (like eczema, allergies, and autoimmune diseases). Make fermented foods a regular part of your diet to help restore good bacteria and prevent a leaky gut. Raw and unpasteurized sauerkraut is delicious and provides the most probiotics, but it can be expensive. Making your own at home is time-consuming, but it's economical and gives you the freedom to customize your recipe just the way you like it.

CABBAGE AND YOUR THYROID

Cabbage is a goitrogenic food, which means that it interferes with thyroid function by inhibiting the absorption of iodine and slowing production of thyroid hormones. Assuming you have a healthy thyroid, you'd have to eat an awful lot of cabbage to notice an effect, so it's not a problem for most people. If you eat cabbage regularly, or if you do have a thyroid problem, just make sure you also get enough iodine by using iodized salt or eating seafood (especially shellfish) or seaweed about twice a week.

BONUS RECIPE

SIMPLE RAW SAUERKRAUT

1 large head green cabbage, sliced into thin strips (set aside two large outer leaves)

1 tablespoon (18 g) unrefined sea salt

Place one-third of the sliced cabbage into a large bowl and sprinkle 1 teaspoon of the salt over the cabbage. Using your hands, squeeze and stir the cabbage until some of the water is released. The cabbage should seem wet. Repeat this process with the remaining cabbage and salt two more times.

Fill 2 large glass mason jars with the cabbage mixture, pressing the mixture down so that the water releases and covers the cabbage. Continue until the jars are filled, leaving about 2 inches (5 cm) of space at the top. Place one of the reserved cabbage leaves on top of the cabbage mixture in each of the jars. The liquid should rise up above the leaf. Then place a shot glass or another heavy object on top of the leaves to keep the cabbage mixture submerged.

Set the filled jars on a plate or baking sheet (something with an edge) to contain any spillover. Place in a secure location at room temperature for at least 2 weeks, sampling periodically to see whether it has fermented to your taste. Once it's ready, screw the lid on the jars and refrigerate to stop the fermenting process. Sauerkraut will last for several months in the refrigerator.

MAKES 32 OUNCES (1 KG)

SUPER COLESLAW

This slaw earns its name because it's packed with many of the
Paleo superfoods you'll find in this book, making it a pretty powerful dish.

To a large bowl add the cabbage, Brussels sprouts, carrot, parsley, scallions, shredded coconut, and sunflower seeds, tossing to combine. Set aside.

In a small bowl whisk together the apple cider vinegar, olive oil, Dijon mustard, ginger, paprika, sea salt, garlic powder, and pepper. Pour over the slaw and stir well. Serve immediately, or refrigerate for a few hours to allow the flavors to develop.

The slaw will keep in an airtight container for 2 to 3 days in the refrigerator.

MAKES 4 OR 5 SERVINGS

½ small savory cabbage, finely shredded

1 cup (88 g) trimmed and finely shredded Brussels sprouts

1 carrot, shredded

¼ cup (16 g) fresh parsley, chopped

2 scallions, finely chopped

¼ cup (20 g) unsweetened dried coconut, shredded

¼ cup (36 g) sunflower seeds

¼ cup (60 ml) apple cider vinegar

2 tablespoons (30 ml) olive oil

1 tablespoon (11 g) Dijon mustard

1 ½ teaspoons grated fresh ginger

½ teaspoon paprika

½ teaspoon sea salt

¼ teaspoon garlic powder

¼ teaspoon black pepper

SPIRULINA

Spirulina, one of the oldest life forms on earth, might be the original superfood. And this ancient, nutrient-dense food is an important part of a Paleo diet. A blue-green microalgae, spirulina helps produce oxygen in our atmosphere and contains an astonishing array of nutrients, which scientists believe made early life possible. In addition to a surprising amount of protein, spirulina provides iron; potassium; vitamin A (in the form of beta-carotene); most of the B vitamins; vitamins C, E, and K; and even some omega-3 fatty acids.

Although spirulina has been around for billions of years, researchers have only studied it for the past fifty years or so. Up until now, most of the studies have focused on spirulina's effects on animals and cell cultures in the laboratory, but evidence from early human trials is promising. Here are some of the ways spirulina earns its place on the list of Paleo superfoods.

FUEL FOR YOUR WORKOUTS

Just 1 tablespoon (8 g) of spirulina provides a remarkable 4 grams of high-quality, complete protein, meaning it contains all eight essential amino acids (the ones your body can't make on its own), plus ten additional amino acids. These amino acids build, repair, and maintain cells and tissues throughout your body—especially helping to mend tiny tears in your muscle fibers after you exercise, increasing muscle strength—and act like building blocks to construct and replenish protein.

A handful of small studies in humans suggest that consuming spirulina daily for several weeks can help you exercise longer and harder. In one double-blind, placebo-controlled crossover study (the gold standard of research methodology), nine moderately fit men took spirulina for four weeks and then completed a treadmill test. The researchers noted that after spirulina supplementation, the men took longer to fatigue and showed "a significant increase in exercise performance." That makes spirulina a perfect superfood if you've incorporated strenuous physical activity into your Paleo lifestyle.

AN ABUNDANCE OF ANTIOXIDANTS

Spirulina contains a variety of flavonoids—antioxidant plant pigments that quench free radicals and protect your cells from oxidative damage. Spirulina gets its blue-green color from a powerful trio of chlorophyll (green), carotenoids (yellow and orange), and phycocyanin (blue). Much of the research on chlorophyll has investigated how it might help protect against cancer. The carotenoids include beta-carotene, which your body converts into vitamin A, and lutein and zeaxanthin, the primary carotenoids in your eyes. These carotenoids work together to help protect your eyes against the effects of aging, such as cataracts and age-related macular degeneration. And phycocyanins help calm inflammation.

Spirulina provides another noteworthy antioxidant: superoxide dismutase (SOD). Abundant throughout your body, SOD is an enzyme that breaks down toxic molecules called superoxide radicals. Superoxide radicals are created during normal cell processes, but they need to be broken down regularly because if too many accumulate, they can damage your cells. Over time, that oxidative damage can lead to chronic diseases such as osteoporosis, type 2 diabetes, neurodegenerative diseases, cardiovascular disease, and cancer, according to a 2012 review in the *Annals of Nutrition and Metabolism*.

A BOOST FOR YOUR IMMUNE SYSTEM

Lab and animal studies indicate that spirulina can help regulate immunity—both by strengthening a weak immune system and by calming an overactive one—possibly by increasing the production of antibodies, infection-fighting proteins, and other cells that improve immunity and protect you against infection and chronic illnesses. Early evidence suggests that spirulina prevents viruses such as the flu, measles, mumps, and HIV from replicating, which means that it can help protect you even after you've been infected. Spirulina also shows promise in treating allergies by inhibiting the release of histamine—in one 2008 study, Turkish researchers found that spirulina significantly improved allergy symptoms, including nasal discharge, sneezing, nasal congestion, and itching, compared with a placebo. More (and larger) studies are needed to verify these effects, but in the research that has been done, spirulina seems to be safe and well tolerated.

SPIRULINA: FROM ANCIENT TO SPACE AGE

Although hunter-gatherer societies have been consuming spirulina since prehistoric times, this blue-green algae lost its prominence in our food supply over the centuries. Spirulina owes its resurgence in popularity to NASA and the European Space Agency, which proposed it as a dietary supplement for astronauts on long-term space missions in the late 1980s and early 1990s.

SHOPPING FOR SPIRULINA

You can find spirulina as a powder, flakes, or tablets. Admittedly, spirulina doesn't have the most pleasant taste by itself, but you can easily camouflage it by adding it to smoothies and other liquid-containing foods such as soups and sauces, and even guacamole. Wild-harvested spirulina is likely to be contaminated with bacteria, liver poisons (microcystins) produced by certain bacteria, and heavy metals, but farming practices are better able to control those environmental toxins. Regardless of the source of the spirulina, be sure to check that the brand you purchase has been tested for safety and purity.

SUPER GREEN SMOOTHIE

Spirulina is a great ingredient in smoothies, especially for those who need a burst of energy during the day. Packed full of antioxidants and crammed with vitamins, it has some amazing health benefits. It isn't for everyone's taste, so I like to sneak it into a delicious, healthy smoothie.

Juice of 2 small lemons

¾ cup (180 ml) filtered water

1 frozen banana, cut into slices

⅔ cup (110 g) pineapple cubes, frozen

¼ avocado, cubed

2 cups (60 g) baby spinach

1 teaspoon spirulina

1 teaspoon honey (optional)

1 teaspoon minced fresh ginger (optional)

Combine all the ingredients in a blender and process until smooth. Pour and serve immediately.

MAKES 3 SERVINGS

TIP:

Have fun with this smoothie and add other frozen fruits such as mango, strawberries, blueberries, raspberries, or blackberries. You can even swap out the spinach for another Paleo super green, kale. Get creative and have fun.

3
PALEO SUPER VEGETABLES AND ROOTS

Green vegetables get a lot of positive press, but the (nongreen) veggies in this chapter are nutritional standouts as well. Even the lowly root vegetables—whose carbohydrates are a source of contention within the Paleo community—have a lot to offer.

First, let's address the carbohydrate issue. Root vegetables are starchy and full of carbs, true. However, the complex carbohydrates and fiber that they offer act quite differently in your body than the refined flours and sugars that are responsible for so many modern health problems, such as obesity, diabetes, and high triglyceride levels, that put you at risk for heart disease. Your body requires carbohydrates for energy, and evidence indicates that many hunter-gatherer societies relied on the high-quality carbohydrates in root vegetables to sustain their intense activity levels. So if you exercise frequently, roots are ideal Paleo superfoods to give you steady energy for powering through and recovering from your workouts.

But there's more to this chapter than just root vegetables. Squash, cauliflower, bell peppers, zucchini, tomatoes—each offers a unique blend of nutrients and antioxidants that make it a Paleo superfood in its own right. From alpha-carotene to zeaxanthin, these vegetables provide an astonishing array of antioxidants that protect your cells from free-radical damage, benefiting nearly every part of your body, from your eyes to your heart to your skin. Color is a good indicator of which antioxidants a vegetable contains, which is why you've probably heard that you should make your plate as colorful as possible. The Paleo superfoods in this chapter will help you do just that.

SWEET POTATOES

Paleo proponents have long debated whether sweet potatoes and other starchy root vegetables are Paleo or not. At issue is their high carbohydrate content. Our modern diets are typically quite high in carbohydrates, especially refined flours and sugars, and that's gotten us into a lot of trouble, healthwise. So many people, understandably, want to limit their carbohydrate intake to help improve conditions like diabetes and other blood sugar disorders, cardiovascular disease, and systemic inflammation.

But there is plenty of evidence that root vegetables were dietary staples for some hunter-gatherer groups, and as long as you're active—like those hunter-gatherers were—you should be fine including sweet potatoes and other starchy vegetables as part of a Paleo lifestyle. The reason is that starch acts differently in your body than the simple sugars such as fructose found in fruits and honey. Your digestive system breaks down starch into glucose, which all of your cells use for energy (and which makes sweet potatoes good fuel for high-powered workouts). Fructose, on the other hand, appears to change the way your brain responds to hunger cues, possibly leading to overeating. Sweet potatoes have the added benefit of being high in fiber (one medium sweet potato contains nearly 4 grams), which gives you a steady and sustained flow of energy instead of a sudden rush.

Of course, carbohydrates aren't the only thing sweet potatoes have to offer. These delicious root vegetables also boast high levels of vitamin A, potassium, and vitamin B_6, and smaller amounts of vitamins C and E.

THE IDEAL EXERCISE RECOVERY FOOD

If, like many Paleo followers, you've increased your activity levels, sweet potatoes will help you get more out of your workouts. During a bout of intense exercise, your muscles use up glycogen (your body's main storage mechanism for energy-producing glucose). Refilling your glycogen stores post-workout will help you recover faster by repairing the tiny muscle tears you create during exercise and by strengthening your muscles. Studies show that the best way to replenish glycogen is by consuming carbohydrates within an hour or two of exercising. Including a little bit of protein ensures that you have enough amino acids to build muscle protein and prevent protein breakdown, according to a 2010 study in the *International Journal*

INCLUDE PALEO-FRIENDLY FATS

Sweet potatoes contain vitamins, such as beta-carotene and vitamin E, that are fat-soluble, which means that consuming them with some fat greatly increases your body's ability to absorb and use them. As little as 3 to 5 grams of fat may do the trick, according to a 2002 study in the journal *Nutrition Reviews*. My favorite way to do this is to peel and dice a large sweet potato, then sauté in 1 tablespoon (14 g) of coconut oil until the sweet potato cubes are tender and slightly golden. Sprinkle with a little sea salt, and you have a great side dish option.

of Sport Nutrition and Exercise Metabolism. One medium sweet potato provides 23 grams of high-quality carbohydrates and 2.3 grams of protein to aid your recovery and make your workout even more effective.

CARDIOVASCULAR HEALTH

Sweet potatoes provide plenty of heart-protective potassium—542 milligrams in one medium potato, or a little more than 10 percent of the recommended daily allowance. Potassium acts as an electrolyte, conducting electricity through your body and regulating your heart's rhythm. Potassium also helps lower blood pressure by improving blood flow, regulating fluid balance, and eliminating excess sodium. And getting enough potassium from foods reduces your risk of heart disease and stroke, according to a 2011 study in the *Journal of the American College of Cardiology.*

One medium sweet potato also contains about one-quarter of the vitamin B_6 you need daily—and high dietary intake of B_6 reduces your risk of stroke, coronary heart disease, and heart failure, notes a 2010 study in the journal *Stroke.* Researchers suspect this is partly because vitamin B_6 helps maintain normal levels of homocysteine in the blood, a marker of inflammation that can indicate risk of cardiovascular disease.

SHOPPING FOR SWEET POTATOES

Although sweet potatoes are available year-round, winter is peak season for these root vegetables. There are many varieties of sweet potatoes. While the most common have yellow-orange or cream-colored flesh, you may also find sweet potatoes that have pink or deep purple skin and flesh. (The color indicates which antioxidant plant pigments are present—the familiar orange sweet potatoes are rich in beta-carotene, while purple potatoes contain anthocyanins.)

These tubers can also vary in shape—some are short and blocky with rounded ends, and others are longer with tapered ends. Choose organically grown sweet potatoes that are firm and don't have any cracks, bruises, or soft spots. Store them in a cool, dark, and well-ventilated place (not the refrigerator) and they'll keep for up to ten days.

Sweet potato flesh starts to darken when it comes in contact with air, so cook them soon after peeling or cutting. Alternatively, you can put them in a bowl with enough water to cover until you're ready to cook them.

CARIBBEAN CITRUS ROASTED SWEET POTATOES

Sweet potatoes are one of the best ways to get more beta-carotene, an antioxidant the body converts to immunity-boosting vitamin A. This hearty root veggie paired with the warm Caribbean spice blend makes for the perfect comfort food, and it's a great side dish to any meal of the day.

FOR CARIBBEAN CITRUS SPICE BLEND:

1½ tablespoons (9 g) ground allspice

3 tablespoons (7.5 g) minced fresh thyme leaves

1½ teaspoons sweet paprika

1 tablespoon (6 g) orange zest

½ teaspoon ground cinnamon

½ teaspoon ground cloves

½ teaspoon ground nutmeg

FOR SWEET POTATOES:

1 large or 2 small sweet potato, peeled

2 tablespoons (12 g) Caribbean Citrus Spice Blend

Sea salt and pepper, to taste

2 to 3 tablespoons (28 to 42 g) coconut oil, melted

To make the Caribbean Citrus Spice Blend: Combine all the spice blend ingredients in a small bowl. Store any leftover spice blend in an airtight container.

To make the sweet potatoes: Preheat the oven to 375°F (190°C, or gas mark 5) and prepare a baking sheet with a Silpat liner, foil, or parchment paper (lining your sheet will save you lots of cleanup time), or spray well with nonstick cooking spray. Slice the sweet potato into sticks or chunks. Place the potatoes on the baking sheet, sprinkle with the Caribbean Citrus Spice Blend and salt and pepper to taste, and drizzle with melted coconut oil. Toss the potatoes with your hands to coat evenly. Bake for 30 minutes, then flip them over. Bake for another 10 to 20 minutes, or until nicely browned and tender. Remove from the oven and serve immediately.

Store extras in an airtight container for up to 2 days in the refrigerator and reheat prior to serving as desired (but know that the leftovers will not stay crispy).

MAKE 3 OR 4 SERVINGS

QUICK TIP:

The leftover spice blend works great as a rub for fish or chicken. For every 3 tablespoons (15 g) of spice, add 1 tablespoon (15 ml) of Paleo-friendly oil to help the spice marinate the fish or meat.

WINTER SQUASH

Originating in the Americas, squashes are one of the oldest known crops, dating back 10,000 years by some estimates based on seeds found in sites in Mexico. Pre-Columbian Indians in both South and North America later made the seeds and flesh a dietary staple. Surprisingly nutritious, these super-foods are a great addition to a Paleo diet, especially in the dead of winter when few other vegetables are in season. They're a good source of vitamins A and C and the B vitamins, plus potassium, fiber, and antioxidants. And the wide variety of squashes and preparation methods—you can steam, boil, mash, purée, roast, bake, or stuff them—ensures you'll never get bored.

ANTIOXIDANT DEFENSE

Winter squashes' yellow-orange flesh is a clue to their high carotenoid content. These antioxidant plant pigments (especially beta-carotene) calm harmful inflammation, helping accomplish one of the main goals of the Paleo diet. Carotenoids also protect the DNA in your cells against free radical damage that can cause ailments ranging from cancer and heart disease to cataracts and arthritis. The more intense the color of the flesh—as with butternut squash's bright orange hue—the more carotenoids are present.

Several kinds of winter squash, including acorn and butternut, provide good amounts of antioxidant vitamin C as well. Some studies indicate that getting enough vitamin C in your diet can slow the progres-sion of atherosclerosis (hardening of the arteries) by preventing free radical damage to LDL ("bad") cholesterol, making it less likely to form plaques in your blood vessels that can trigger a heart attack or

stroke. Population studies indicate that eating foods rich in antioxidants, including vitamin C, also reduces your risk of high blood pressure.

BLOOD SUGAR BENEFITS

The Paleo diet is exceptionally good at helping regulate blood sugar levels, partly thanks to foods such as winter squashes. These humble veggies contain complex carbohydrates called polysaccharides that help regulate your blood sugar, which not only reduces your risk of developing type 2 diabetes but also protects you against other symptoms of out-of-control blood sugar, including unbalanced hormones, energy crashes, altered metabolism, and weakened thyroid function. All varieties of winter squash supply dietary fiber, which fills you up and slows digestion to prevent your blood sugar from spiking and crashing after you eat. But they also contain a polysaccharide starch that your body digests and absorbs gradually so it similarly won't cause a spike (and subsequent crash) in your blood sugar levels. That makes winter squashes a great source of slow-burning carbs that your body needs for long-lasting energy, whether you're powering through an intense workout or just a hectic day.

VARIETIES

Winter squashes come in a wide range of shapes, sizes, colors, and flavors, but many of them can be used interchangeably in recipes. Here are some of the kinds you're most likely to find at your local market.

ACORN: Named for its distinct shape, this small squash has wide ribs and dark green, gold, or white thick skin. Its sweet yellow or orange flesh turns creamy when cooked.

BUTTERNUT SQUASH: Large and bell-shaped with a creamy rind and deep orange, sweet flesh, this popular squash boasts the highest vitamin A and C content of nearly all the varieties.

CALABAZA: Popular in the Caribbean and Central and South America, these round squashes have very tough rinds that come in colors ranging from tan to green to reddish orange. The firm flesh tastes similar to butternut squash.

DELICATA: These are oblong in shape with a thin, pale yellow skin and dark green pinstripes. Its yellow flesh is reminiscent of sweet potatoes and butternut squash and can be prepared in similar ways. The skin is thin enough that you don't need to peel it before cooking.

HUBBARD: One of the largest winter varieties, these round squashes have brightly colored, nubby rinds ranging from orange to green to grayish blue. Its yellow or orange flesh is both savory and sweet but a bit grainy; try it mashed or puréed.

KABOCHA: Shaped like a pumpkin (and similar in flavor), this Japanese squash has dark green skin and light green striations. Its sweet, almost fiberless flesh makes it versatile—use it for cooking or baking.

PUMPKIN: This bright orange fall staple works well in baking (hence its popularity in pie), but the mellow, dense, sweet flesh is also delicious in savory dishes. Choose pumpkins that weigh about 2 to 5 pounds (908 to 2270 g).

SPAGHETTI: This oval yellow squash contains a stringy flesh that, when cooked, separates into mild-tasting spaghetti-like strands that make a great Paleo-friendly pasta substitute.

SHOPPING FOR WINTER SQUASH

As you might expect from their name, winter squashes are at their peak in the cold-weather months. When shopping, look for squash that are firm and heavy for their size and have dull, hard rinds. Avoid any squashes that have soft spots or areas that are water-soaked or moldy. Many varieties have a long storage life—kept at room temperature away from direct light, some winter squashes with hard rinds can last for several months. Those with softer rinds, however, may last only a week, so check them often for signs of decay. Once you cut your winter squash, whatever the variety, store it in an airtight container in the refrigerator and use within a few days.

TRY THIS!

Buttercup squash is a small, hard-skinned winter squash with deep yellow flesh and a sweet flavor that is reminiscent of sweet potatoes (in fact, it was developed to make up for a failed sweet potato crop). As such, you can substitute it almost any-where that you would use sweet potatoes.

You can also swap cubes of most varieties of winter squash for cubed white potatoes in ethnic dishes, especially stews and soups, which is a great way to adapt non-Paleo recipes.

And don't throw away the seeds! Roasted and lightly seasoned, most winter squash seeds make a great snack. Rinse the seeds and pat them dry. Then toss them with 1 tablespoon (15 ml) of Paleo-friendly fat, such as coconut oil, sprinkle with a smidge of salt, and roast in a 275°F (140°C, or gas mark 1) oven for 15 minutes, or until tender.

PUMPKIN PANCAKES WITH TOASTED PECANS

Pancakes are a Paleo treat in my house, mostly served on weekends and especially after the request/begging of my six-year-old twins. On a crisp fall morning these pancakes are a favorite to warm the soul (plus, pumpkin's vitamin C can help ward off illness during cold and flu season!). Try switching up the pumpkin purée for sweet potato purée or ripe banana purée.

½ cup (120 g) pumpkin purée

2 eggs

1 tablespoon (14 g) coconut oil, melted, plus more for griddle

2 tablespoons (30 ml) maple syrup

2 tablespoons (30 ml) coconut milk

1 teaspoon vanilla extract

½ cup (60 g) almond flour

1 tablespoon (8 g) coconut flour*

1½ teaspoons ground cinnamon

¼ teaspoon sea salt

¼ teaspoon baking soda

¼ cup (38 g) pecans, chopped

*See Resources, page 214.

Heat a griddle or nonstick skillet over medium heat (watch the temperature carefully to keep the pancakes from burning).

In a large bowl, add the pumpkin, eggs, 1 tablespoon (15 ml) melted coconut oil, maple syrup, coconut milk, and vanilla. Using a hand mixer, combine the ingredients until smooth and blended. Add the almond flour, coconut flour, cinnamon, salt, and baking soda to the wet ingredients and mix again until everything is incorporated.

Melt 1 teaspoon of additional coconut oil in the hot griddle or skillet, making sure the oil coats the surface evenly. Pour about ¼ to ⅓ cup (60 to 80 ml) batter to the skillet for each pancake. Allow the pancakes to cook on one side for 3 to 4 minutes, or until the bottoms are golden. (These don't cook like traditional pancakes, so don't flip the pancakes too soon or they will break apart.) Then, using a spatula, carefully flip the pancakes over to cook on the other side. Repeat with the remaining batter.

While the pancakes cook, preheat the oven to 350°F (180°C, or gas mark 4) and evenly spread the pecans on a baking sheet. Toast the pecans for 5 to 10 minutes, or until lightly toasted and fragrant. Top the pancakes with toasted pecans and serve.

MAKES 5 OR 6 PANCAKES

CARROTS

Crispy, crunchy, and delicious, carrots are one of the most popular vegetables among kids and adults alike. In addition to the familiar orange carrots we know and love, you can find purple, red, yellow, and white varieties around the world, and especially in the Middle East, where domesticated carrots originated thousands of years ago. In fact, orange carrots didn't make an appearance until the 1700s in the Netherlands.

Carrots are naturally sweet, and there is some debate about whether they are acceptable on the Paleo diet. But like other starchy root vegetables, they contain plenty of fiber and polysaccharides to prevent any harmful effects on your blood sugar, while providing a steady source of energy to fuel an active Paleo lifestyle. Because of these benefits, plus their wealth of antioxidants, vitamins, and minerals, I consider carrots a Paleo superfood.

VISION BOOSTER

Yes, your mom was right—eating carrots is a great way to protect your eyesight, especially as you get older. And while they won't replace your glasses, carrots are packed with carotenoids that fight the free radicals that can cause poor night vision, dry eyes, cataracts, and age-related macular degeneration (loss of central vision). Carotenoids are antioxidant plant pigments, and different colors indicate the presence of different antioxidants: orange carrots are high in beta-carotene, yellow carrots have more lutein, red carrots get their color from lycopene, and purple carrots contain higher levels of anthocyanins. Each antioxidant plays its own protective role in your eyes, but beta-carotene is the primary carotenoid in the orange carrots we typically eat.

Your body converts beta-carotene into vitamin A, and just one medium carrot provides 509 retinol activity equivalents (RAE), or nearly 200 percent of the recommended daily amount. Although preformed vitamin A can build up to toxic levels in your body, you can't overdose on the vitamin A that your body converts from beta-carotene, so feel free to munch and crunch on as many carrots as you like. By and large, we already follow that advice—these sweet root vegetables provide 30 percent of the vitamin A in the American diet, according to the U.S. Department of Agriculture.

Your body can absorb and use all the carotenoids more efficiently from carrots that are cooked with a little Paleo-friendly fat, such as coconut oil. But however you cook them—boiled, steamed, roasted, sautéed, stir-fried, or blanched—make sure they still have some crunch so you don't destroy their other nutrients.

FUN FACT

The peeled baby carrots you buy in the supermarket are not actually baby carrots at all—they're full-size carrots that have been peeled and cut. You can find true baby (immature) carrots with their tops still attached at well-stocked supermarkets or farmers' markets.

CANCER PREVENTER

Much of carrots' anticancer protection comes from antioxidants such as carotenoids, lycopene, and anthocyanins. Vitamin A regulates cell growth and division, and consuming foods rich in beta-carotene in particular seems to reduce the risk of specific kinds of cancer such as prostate and lung cancer (though supplements don't seem to be helpful, and may even be harmful). Carrots contain another phytonutrient called polyacetylene that appears to fight cancer as well. In lab studies, several kinds of polyacetylenes seem able to interrupt the life cycle of cancer cells (which keeps them from multiplying) and trigger cell death, especially in leukemia and colon cancer. Additional research will clarify whether these results will translate to humans.

HEART HELPER

Eating dark orange foods such as carrots may reduce your risk of developing heart disease by up to 32 percent, according to a 2011 study in the *British Journal of Nutrition*. Other research suggests that it's the alpha- and beta-carotenes responsible for this effect, and that consuming these antioxidants that give carrots their deep orange color lowers the risk of dying from cardiovascular disease.

SKIN SAVER

Vitamin A is crucial for keeping skin healthy by promoting cell turnover and regulating skin cell growth and differentiation, among other functions. A deficiency can lead to dry, flaky skin, and hyper-keratosis pilaris—rough, raised bumps on the backs of the arms. Topical vitamin A (retinol) is the gold standard treatment for many bothersome skin conditions such as acne, eczema, psoriasis, wounds, burns, and sunburns, but increasing your dietary intake may prove helpful as well. Consuming vitamin A, along with antioxidant vitamins C and E, can help repair skin damage caused by sun exposure and other environmental factors, according to a 2012 study in *Dermatology Research and Practice*.

CARROTS: BUY THE BUNCH

You can find carrots in supermarkets and farmers' markets year-round. Choose organic carrots to avoid toxic pesticide residue (if the carrots at your farmers' market aren't labeled organic, ask the seller about his or her growing practices—many smaller farms don't go through the time-consuming and expensive process to be certified organic, but they may still use organic methods).

Look for firm, intensely colored carrots without splits or cracks. If the leafy tops are attached, they should be bright green, and you should trim them down to 1 inch (2.5 cm) before storing your carrots. Without their tops, carrots will stay fresh in a plastic bag in the crisper drawer of your refrigerator for about two weeks. Don't store your carrots near apples or pears, which give off gasses that turn carrots bitter.

PURPLE HAZE

If you are able to find purple carrots at the market, you should definitely give them a try! They're delicious and besides offering the beta-carotene of traditional orange carrots, they are also rich in anthocyanins, the same antioxidant compounds that give blueberries (and other blue/purple foods) their distinctive color and superfood benefits.

ROASTED LEMON SAGE CARROTS AND PARSNIPS

Roasting parsnips and carrots and accenting them with fresh sage and
lemon transforms these humble vegetables into a delicious side dish. As an added bonus,
the sage and thyme in this dish contribute some vitamin K, a nutrient your body requires for
responding to injuries.

4 large carrots, peeled and cut into
½-inch (1.3 cm) pieces

3 large parsnips, peeled and cut into
½-inch (1.3 cm) pieces

3 fresh thyme sprigs

2 tablespoons (28 g) coconut oil,
melted

Sea salt and freshly ground black
pepper, to taste

5 or 6 sage leaves, chopped

Zest and juice of 1 lemon

Preheat the oven to 400°F (200°C, or gas mark 6). Line a baking sheet
with parchment paper and set aside.

Combine the carrots, parsnips, thyme sprigs, and coconut oil in a large
bowl, tossing to coat the vegetables. Season with salt and pepper. Evenly
spread the carrot and parsnip mixture on the prepared baking sheet.
Roast until the vegetables are tender and lightly browned on top, about
30 minutes.

Remove and discard the thyme sprigs. Toss the vegetables with the sage
and add the lemon zest and lemon juice, to taste. Serve immediately.

MAKES 4 SERVINGS

TIDBIT:

Parsnips are in the root vegetable family and are closely related to carrots. Along with their sweet flavor, parsnips bring vitamin C, folate, and
potassium to the table.

Look for small to medium-size creamy white parsnips that are smooth
and blemish free.

CAULIFLOWER

Cauliflower is a staple in the Paleo diet because it is highly nutritious and incredibly versatile, making it a good substitute for nutrient-poor, high-carbohydrate foods such as white rice or potatoes. You can easily transform these "little white trees" (as my kids call them) into cauliflower rice, cauliflower couscous, and even cauliflower mash. In my house, we just can't get enough cauliflower.

One popular piece of advice we get from nutrition experts is to make your meals as colorful as possible, because color generally indicates the presence of specific health-promoting substances. But while eating a wide variety of vibrantly colored foods certainly is important, don't pass up cauliflower just because it doesn't stand out on your plate. Cauliflower belongs to the family of cruciferous vegetables, which means it packs a similar nutritional punch as its cousins broccoli, cabbage, and Brussels sprouts. But cauliflower is a Paleo superstar in its own right, brimming with antioxidants and anti-inflammatory and detoxifying compounds—hallmarks of the Paleo diet. And this unassuming white vegetable also boasts impressive amounts of vitamin C, vitamin K, several B vitamins, potassium, fiber, and even some omega-3s.

INFLAMMATION TAMER

Although some inflammation is actually helpful—such as when your immune system is fighting off a bug— oftentimes it's just annoying, such as when you're recovering from a strenuous workout, and it can even be dangerous, in the case of chronic inflammation. Chronic inflammation is linked to health problems, including heart disease, rheumatoid arthritis, asthma, and possibly cancer, and it can accelerate the aging process. But cauliflower helps calm that harmful inflammation in several ways.

Lab and population studies indicate that vitamin K can quell inflammation throughout the body, and cauliflower provides 16.6 micrograms per cup (132 g)— 14 percent of what men need and 18 percent of what women need daily. A 2008 study in the *American Journal of Epidemiology* found that people with higher vitamin K levels had lower concentrations of inflammatory markers, even after adjusting for other factors that might have affected inflammation.

Antioxidants in cauliflower fight free radicals that can trigger inflammation as well. One cup (132 g) of raw florets boasts 52 milligrams of vitamin C—well over half of what you need each day. It also contains 0.34 milligram of manganese, a trace mineral that quenches harmful peroxyl radicals. And lest you think that cauliflower doesn't contain antioxidant plant pigments like other brilliantly colored vegetables, rest assured that cauliflower gets its creamy white hue from anthoxanthin, which is every bit as powerful a free radical scavenger as the other flavonoids.

Cauliflower even contains 37 milligrams of inflammation-calming omega-3 fatty acids per cup (132 g). To be sure, that's nowhere near wild salmon's stellar omega-3 content, but every little bit of these protective fats can help get you closer to the Paleo ideal ratio of 2:1 omega-6s to omega-3s.

NATURAL DETOXIFIER

Sulfur-containing compounds called glucosinolates give cauliflower (and other cruciferous veggies) its distinctive smell. The act of chewing cauliflower breaks down glucosinolates into compounds such as sulforaphane that stimulate your natural detoxification enzymes and help rid your body of environmental carcinogens. In fact, evidence suggests that these phytochemicals may reduce the risk of prostate, breast, lung, and colorectal cancer. Intensive cooking can destroy the enzyme that breaks down glucosinolates into their beneficial compounds, so be careful not to overcook cauliflower—just a few minutes of cooking (so that it still retains a bit of crunch) should be sufficient.

One cup (132 g) of cauliflower florets delivers about 2.1 g of dietary fiber, which also promotes detoxification. Fiber speeds the digestive process so your body can excrete waste products and environmental toxins more quickly. Fiber can also discourage the growth of harmful bacteria and help restore and maintain levels of healthy bacteria in your gut.

SELECTING AND COOKING CAULIFLOWER

Cauliflower is in season from December through March, although you can probably find it in markets outside of that time frame. A head of cauliflower, which is called a curd, is actually a cluster of undeveloped flower buds. The thick green leaves that surround the head protect it and keep it fresher (they also shield it from the sun exposure that would otherwise turn it green). When you shop for cauliflower, you'll want to make sure that the curd is a clean, creamy white and that it's compact—so that the bud clusters aren't separated or, worse, starting to flower. Avoid spotted or dull-colored cauliflower, possible indications of mold. When you get it home, store your cauliflower in a paper or plastic bag in the refrigerator, stem side down, to prevent moisture from gathering in the florets and encouraging mold. Uncooked cauliflower should keep for up to a week.

BONUS RECIPE

CAULIFLOWER CARROT HERB MASH

1 head cauliflower, washed and cut into florets

3 or 4 small to medium carrots, peeled and chopped

Salt and pepper to taste

2 tablespoons (30 ml) olive oil, divided

1 sweet onion, chopped

2 cloves garlic, minced

1 tablespoon (1.7 g) fresh rosemary, minced, plus more for garnish

1 tablespoon (2.4 g) fresh thyme, minced, plus more for garnish

Sea salt and freshly ground black pepper, to taste

Place the cauliflower and carrots in a steamer basket in a large soup pot, season with salt and pepper, and steam until soft (about 10 to 12 minutes, test with a fork).

Heat 1 tablespoon (15 ml) of the olive oil in a nonstick skillet over medium heat. Sauté the onion, garlic, and herbs until the onions are translucent, 5 to 10 minutes. Season with salt and pepper to taste. Set aside.

Place the steamed cauliflower and carrots into a food processor. Add the onion mixture and remaining 1 tablespoon (15 ml) olive oil. Process until smooth. Season with more salt and pepper, if desired. Garnish with additional fresh thyme or rosemary, and serve.

MAKES 3 CUPS (560 G)

When you cook cauliflower, keep in mind that it's easy to overcook, which will turn it to mush. Also, avoid cooking it in non-anodized aluminum or iron pots—cauliflower's creamy white anthoxanthin pigments will react with the metals and turn it yellowish (in an aluminum pot) or blue-green or brown (in an iron pot).

CAULIFLOWER "COUSCOUS" VEGGIE SALAD

This light and refreshing salad is the perfect side dish for your summertime cookout, and your guests may not believe that cauliflower is the shining star. Have fun with the vegetables and change them up depending on what is in season to get the greatest nutritional and flavor benefits.

2 tablespoons (28 g) coconut oil (or ghee or bacon grease)

¼ cup (40 g) chopped yellow onion

2 celery stalks, finely diced

1 head cauliflower, trimmed and coarsely chopped

½ cup (50 g) thinly sliced scallion

½ cup (80 g) diced red bell pepper

½ cup (75 g) halved cherry tomatoes

½ cup (60 g) diced cucumber

¼ cup (15 g) fresh parsley, chopped

3 tablespoons (7.5 g) fresh basil, chopped

¼ cup (60 ml) fresh lemon juice (about 2 to 3 lemons)

3 tablespoons (45 ml) olive oil

1 medium clove garlic, minced

¼ teaspoon sea salt

¼ teaspoon freshly ground black pepper

In a large skillet, warm the coconut oil over medium heat. Once it's hot, add the onion and sauté for 5 minutes, or until soft and tender. Add the celery and sauté for an additional 5 minutes.

Meanwhile, place the cauliflower florets in a food processor and process until the texture resembles couscous. Add the cauliflower to the skillet; cover and cook for 5 to 10 minutes, or until soft.

Remove from the heat and let cool to room temperature. The couscous can be made a day in advance and stored in the refrigerator before adding the remaining ingredients.

In a large bowl, combine the scallion, red bell pepper, tomatoes, cucumber, parsley, and basil and toss gently. Add the cauliflower couscous to the bowl and mix to incorporate with the vegetables.

In a small bowl whisk together the lemon juice, olive oil, garlic, sea salt, and black pepper. Pour the dressing over the cauliflower mixture and toss to combine.

Serve immediately. Leftovers can be stored in an airtight container in the refrigerator for up to 3 days.

MAKES 6 TO 8 SERVINGS

BELL PEPPERS

Bell peppers have a sweet, tangy flavor and offer a bounty of health benefits. Available in a variety of colors (most commonly green, red, orange, and yellow), bell peppers are a rich source of important vitamins, minerals, and antioxidants. Although botanically they fall into the fruit category, most people consider them vegetables and use them that way in cooking.

NUTRIENTS FOR A HEALTHY HEART

Yes, you've given up grains and legumes on the Paleo diet, but you can still get plenty of cholesterol-clearing fiber in vegetables such as bell peppers—1 cup (150 g) of chopped bell pepper provides about 3 grams. Bell peppers also provide potassium for healthy muscle function (including your heart), and magnesium, which helps maintain a normal heart rhythm. All three nutrients help lower high blood pressure as well, notes a 2000 review in the *British Journal of Nutrition*.

Bell peppers also contain good amounts of most of the B vitamins, which can help reduce your risk of heart attack and stroke. Several B vitamins improve blood flow and help produce red blood cells. And a deficiency in B_2 (riboflavin), B_6, or folate may raise your levels of homocysteine, an inflammatory marker linked to heart disease. The Bs also help convert blood sugar into energy, fueling an active Paleo lifestyle that further reduces your risk of cardiovascular problems.

AN ABUNDANCE OF ANTIOXIDANTS

Cup for cup, bell peppers contain more vitamin C than oranges (in fact, red bell peppers have more than twice the vitamin C!). They're also good sources of antioxidant vitamin A, thanks to their beta-carotene. Different colored peppers boast higher levels of the various phytochemicals that give them their brilliant colors—red peppers owe their hue to lycopene, orange to alpha- and beta-carotenes, and green and yellow peppers to lutein and zeaxanthin. These plant compounds boost your immune system and fight cell-damaging free radicals that put you at risk for heart disease, cancer, and chronic inflammation, and speed the aging process.

NIGHTSHADE PLANTS

Bell peppers belong to the nightshade (*Solanaceae*) family, which also includes foods such as eggplant, potatoes, and tomatoes. Some people are especially sensitive to nightshades' high alkaloid content and experience stomach discomfort, digestive difficulties, joint pain, or muscle tremors after eating them. If you suspect that nightshades cause problems for you (for example, if you have GERD, gout, or arthritis), try eliminating them for a few weeks to see whether your symptoms improve. Cooking nightshades can reduce their alkaloid levels by 40 to 50 percent.

SOUTHWESTERN BEEF AND PEPPER MEDLEY

Mostly thanks to the bell peppers, this recipe is an incredible source of vitamin C, with a single serving providing more than 200% of your recommended daily intake. Try serving this with fresh guacamole or diced avocado.

In a small bowl, stir together the chili powder, half the sea salt, paprika, onion powder, cumin, garlic powder, and cayenne pepper. Set aside.

Cut the skirt steak with the grain into 3-inch (7.5 cm) pieces, then cut each piece across the grain into ¼-inch (6 mm) slices. Place the steak pieces in a large bowl and sprinkle the spice mixture over; toss to coat. Let stand at room temperature for 15 minutes.

In a large bowl, combine the onion and bell peppers and toss with the melted coconut oil. Season with the remaining sea salt and toss to coat.

Heat a large skillet over medium-high heat. Add the vegetables and cook until the peppers soften, about 10 to 12 minutes, tossing occasionally. Transfer to a bowl and set aside.

Add the skirt steak to the skillet in a single layer and cook for 2 to 3 minutes. Then flip the steak pieces and cook for an additional 2 to 3 minutes, or until well browned. Return the vegetables to the skillet, sprinkle with the chopped cilantro, and toss well to combine. Serve immediately.

MAKES 4 TO 6 SERVINGS

1 teaspoon chili powder

½ teaspoon sea salt, divided

½ teaspoon paprika

½ teaspoon onion powder

½ teaspoon ground cumin

¼ teaspoon garlic powder

⅛ teaspoon ground cayenne pepper

1½ pounds (680 g) grass-fed skirt steak

½ large red onion, diced

1 red bell pepper, cored, seeded, and thinly sliced into strips

1 yellow bell pepper, cored, seeded, and thinly sliced into strips

1 green bell pepper, cored, seeded, and thinly sliced into strips

1 tablespoon (28 g) coconut oil, melted

⅓ cup (5 g) fresh cilantro, chopped

TIDBIT:

Available year-round, bell peppers are at their best during the summer and early fall months. Opt for organic whenever possible; bell peppers occupy a spot on the Environmental Working Group's Dirty Dozen list of foods most contaminated by pesticide residue. Choose organic peppers with green, fresh-looking stems and tight, unblemished skin. Peppers should be firm, yielding only slightly to light pressure, and heavy for their size. Bell peppers will keep, refrigerated, for up to ten days.

TOMATOES

Like bell peppers, tomatoes are fruits that we tend to use like vegetables and are also members of the nightshade family (see page 102 for more on nightshades). Possibly because of their association with poisonous nightshade, tomatoes didn't become popular to eat until the late sixteenth century in Italy. In the years since, however, tomatoes and tomato products have become dietary staples the world over. Tomatoes are the most-consumed non-starchy "vegetable" in the American diet, and also the richest source of the antioxidant lycopene. Lycopene is a red plant pigment in the category of antioxidants called carotenoids, which also include alpha- and beta-carotenes, lutein, and zeaxanthin. Tomatoes' high concentration of lycopene earns them a spot on the Paleo superfood list, but they contain good amounts of important Paleo nutrients such as antioxidant vitamins C and E, vitamin K, potassium, and fiber as well.

CARDIOVASCULAR SUPPORT

Antioxidants in tomatoes, including vitamins C and E, the carotenoids, and lycopene, protect your cardiovascular health in several ways. These antioxidants work to prevent oxygen damage to fats in your cell membranes and bloodstream (a process called lipid peroxidation that can lead to atherosclerosis and other cardiovascular problems). Lycopene in particular may help lower blood pressure and, in one study, was as effective as low-dose statin drugs in lowering total and LDL ("bad") cholesterol in people with slightly elevated levels, according to a 2011 review in the journal *Maturitas*.

Research reveals that lycopene can help protect you against stroke as well. In a 2012 study that followed more than 1,000 Finnish men, those who had the highest concentrations of lycopene in their blood had a 55 percent lower risk of any kind of stroke than those who had the lowest levels (the numbers are even more impressive—a 59 percent risk reduction—for strokes caused by blood clots, the most common kind). Surprisingly, other antioxidants, including alpha-carotene, beta-carotene, vitamin A, and vitamin E, had no effect on stroke risk.

The potassium in tomatoes also plays a role in protecting your cardiovascular system. Studies show that increasing your potassium intake can reduce your risk of dying from cardiovascular disease, possibly by keeping your blood pressure in check. Our Stone Age ancestors ate a diet of fresh meats, vegetables, and fruits that contained up to ten times as much potassium as it did sodium, notes a 2002 study in the *Journal of the American Nutraceutical Association*. The average American diet, on the other hand, provides about twice as much sodium as potassium—an imbalance that contributes to high blood pressure and increases your risk of stroke. Eating tomatoes can help correct that imbalance.

BOOST TOMATOES' BENEFITS

You'll get the most out of your tomatoes if you serve them cooked and with a little Paleo-friendly fat. Heat breaks down tomatoes' cell walls to make their carotenoids and flavonoids—including lycopene—more available. That means that canned and jarred tomato products are still a great choice when fresh tomatoes aren't in season.

Carotenoids are also fat-soluble, which means that consuming tomatoes with a little bit of fat increases your ability to absorb these antioxidants. (This becomes especially important when you're eating raw tomatoes, such as in salads or salsas.)

CONQUERING CANCER

Studies suggest that lycopene can help prevent cancer, most likely due to its powerful antioxidant capabilities. Lycopene's unique molecular shape makes it especially effective at quenching a wide variety of cell-damaging free radicals, notes Edward Giovannucci, M.D., Sc.D., a professor of nutrition and epidemiology at the Harvard School of Public Health. In fact, out of all the carotenoids, lycopene is the best at scavenging a specific kind of harmful free radical called singlet oxygen.

Much of the existing research has focused on lycopene's effect on prostate cancer, but some evidence indicates it may protect against other kinds, such as breast, colon, and gastric cancer, as well. A 2012 study in the journal *Cancer Cell International* tested lycopene's effect on several different types of cancer cells and found that the antioxidant was particularly good at stopping prostate, breast, and colon cancer cell proliferation, stopping the cell life cycle in different stages, and causing those cells to die.

TOMATO TUTORIAL

Several studies show that organically grown tomatoes provide more antioxidant plant compounds than conventional tomatoes. In fact, after studying samples from a ten-year period for flavonoid content, researchers found that organic tomatoes boasted a whopping 79 percent more quercetin and 97 percent more kaempferol than their conventional counterparts, according to a 2007 study in the *Journal of Agricultural and Food Chemistry*.

Plus, organic tomatoes just taste better! Other factors that affect the taste include buying them in season (July and August) and locally—so that they're grown for flavor and not their ability to survive long shipping distances. Whether you choose the traditional red or a wildly colored heirloom variety, the skin should be smooth, with no wrinkles, bruises, or open cracks (heirloom tomatoes are more prone to cracks, but as long as you can't see the flesh, they shouldn't affect the taste). Cold temperatures turn tomatoes mealy, so store them at room temperature, out of direct sunlight. Depending on how ripe they are, tomatoes may keep for up to a week.

FRITTATA WITH TOMATOES, ZUCCHINI, AND BASIL

Protein-packed frittatas are a great, hearty dish that can be made for any meal of the day. They are also quick and simple and can be on the table in no time. Possibly the best thing about them (other than the taste, of course!) is how adaptable they are to whatever ingredients you have on hand.

1 tablespoon (14 g) coconut oil (or bacon grease or ghee)

2 medium zucchini, cut into rounds and quartered

2 scallions, finely diced

1 tablespoon (1 g) fresh basil, chopped

1 cup (150 g) cherry tomatoes, halved

Sea salt and freshly ground black pepper

10 large eggs

Preheat the oven to 425°F (220°C, or gas mark 7).

In a 10-inch (25 cm) ovenproof skillet over medium heat, warm the oil. Add the zucchini; cook, covered, stirring often, until tender, about 3 to 5 minutes. Uncover and add the scallions, basil, and tomatoes and cook until all the liquid in the pan evaporates, about 2 to 3 minutes. Season with salt and pepper; remove the skillet from the heat.

In a medium bowl, whisk the eggs. Pour the eggs over the zucchini mixture, gently lifting the vegetables to allow the eggs to coat the bottom of the pan.

Return the skillet to medium-low heat, and cook until the sides are set yet still slightly runny on top, 15 to 20 minutes. Place in the oven, and cook until the center is cooked through when tested with a wooden toothpick, about 10 to 15 minutes. Remove from the oven; gently slide a heatproof spatula around the edges and underneath to loosen it from the skillet. Serve immediately.

MAKES 6 TO 8 SERVINGS

ZUCCHINI

Fossil evidence of seeds indicates that squashes such as zucchini have been around for more than 10,000 years, originating in Mexico and Central America. A member of the summer squash family, this prolific grower is a Paleo superfood staple during the warmer months. Zucchini is a natural on the grill, but you can also shred it into salads, dice it into soups and sauces, slice it into stir-fries and casseroles, stuff it with meat or vegetables, or use strips as Paleo "pasta."

PRIMAL WORKOUT FUEL

If you live an active lifestyle like many Paleo followers do, start piling zucchini on your plate—it contains several nutrients that help you power through your workouts. In addition to its muscle-building protein, this summer squash boasts B vitamins that convert blood sugar into energy; play a role in metabolizing the fats, proteins, and carbohydrates you consume; and help produce amino acid proteins.

Zucchini offers magnesium and potassium to keep your muscles healthy and working at optimum levels (they're critical for smooth muscle contraction). When you exercise, you lose magnesium and potassium in your sweat, but eating zucchini after a workout can help replenish these valuable electrolytes.

FROM Z(UCCHINI) TO A(NTIOXIDANTS)

Like so many of the veggie Paleo superfoods, zucchini is a great source of antioxidants, which scavenge free radicals that damage your cells, accelerating the aging process and contributing to a whole host of relatively modern health problems such as chronic inflammation, heart disease, and cancer. Many of zucchini's antioxidants are in its bright green peel, including lutein and zeaxanthin, which protect your eyes from developing vision problems such as cataracts. A 2012 study in the journal *Ophthalmology* found that lutein and zeaxanthin improved vision and seemed to slow the progression of early age-related macular degeneration (the leading cause of blindness in people over age fifty).

Zucchini also delivers about one-third of the antioxidant vitamin C you need each day, and it's a good source of vitamin A (thanks to its carotenoids). Zucchini supplies more than 10 percent of your daily requirement of the trace mineral manganese as well, which helps your cells adapt to oxidative stress.

SHOPPING FOR SQUASH

Purchase organic zucchini whenever possible (conventional zucchini likely carries traces of organochlorine pesticides that are highly toxic to the nervous system, according to the Environmental Working Group). Look for zucchini that are heavy for their size with tender, shiny, unblemished rinds. Zucchini are fragile, but they will keep, unwashed, in an airtight container in the refrigerator for up to one week.

SPRING VEGGIE PALEO PASTA

Who says pasta is out the door while eating Paleo? Enjoy this nutrient-rich spring pasta and you'll never miss the old stuff. This is also great served with salmon, shrimp, scallops, or the protein of your choice.

Begin by cutting off the ends of the zucchini and washing them. Using a vegetable peeler, peel one side at a time to make 4 ribbons, then rotate and make another 4 ribbons. Continue to rotate and peel until you hit the core of seeds, then stop. Save the core to dice up in another recipe. Do this for both zucchini and the yellow squash; you should have a large bowl of ribbons, depending on the size of your squashes.

In a pan over medium-low heat, melt 1 tablespoon (14 g) of the ghee. Dump in your ribbons (you may need to do this in batches depending on how many ribbons you have and the size of your pan—don't overcrowd it). Stir constantly with a spoon and allow the ribbons to cook through and wilt a little, about 1 to 2 minutes (be careful not to overcook).

In a separate skillet over medium heat, melt the remaining ½ tablespoon (7 g) ghee and add the tomatoes and asparagus, stirring until cooked and tender, about 3 to 4 minutes. Add the diced scallion and basil in the last 30 seconds of cooking and season with salt and pepper to taste.

Place the squash ribbon "pasta" in a bowl and top with the veggie mixture. Sprinkle with additional basil and scallions and serve as a side dish or top with the protein of your choice to make a main course.

MAKES 2 TO 4 SERVINGS

2 organic zucchini

1 organic yellow squash

1½ tablespoons (21 g) ghee (or bacon grease, coconut oil, or olive oil), divided

½ cup (75 g) cherry tomatoes, halved

1 bunch asparagus, chopped

1 or 2 scallions, diced, plus more for garnish

2 tablespoons (5 g) fresh basil, chopped, plus more for garnish

Sea salt and freshly ground pepper to taste

THE SQUASH OF SUMMER

Zucchini is the most common summer squash, but other varieties include yellow, pattypan, crookneck, sunburst, chayote, and opo. Because they're harvested when they're immature, all parts of summer squash are edible, including the flesh, seeds, and skin. Some summer squash (including zucchini) also produce edible flowers.

4
PALEO SUPER FRUITS

There's some debate about how much—and what kinds—of fruit you should eat as part of the Paleo diet, largely because of the varying amounts of naturally occurring sugars that fruits contain. Everybody processes carbohydrates (including those natural sugars) differently, and your activity levels make a big difference in how many carbohydrates your body needs, so it's hard to make a blanket statement about how much fruit is okay. Certainly, early hunter-gatherers ate fruit, and our bodies are generally well adapted to processing the sugars it contains. Fruit also contains a wealth of vitamins, minerals, phytochemicals, and fiber that benefit your health. However, the wild fruit available thousands of years ago tended to be smaller, higher in fiber, and less sweet than the fruit commonly available today.

For many people just starting the Paleo diet, it makes sense to consume fruit conservatively—maybe one serving a day of low-sugar fruits like many of those listed in this chapter—until you see how your body responds. (You can still get plenty of healthy carbohydrates from vegetables, nuts, and seeds.) If you are very much overweight or have insulin resistance, you may need to continue limiting your fruit consumption until your weight comes down and your body is better able to keep your blood sugar in check. At that point, you are free to experiment with the quantity and types of fruits that you eat, again, paying close attention to how your body feels. For example, I really like to eat fruit, especially in the warmer summer months, but I limit the amount of fruit I eat to one serving per day, usually in the mornings or after a workout. But some people may be able to tolerate more—your body will tell you.

In general, stick to fruit that is in season, organic, and locally grown, if possible. Some of the vitamins and health-promoting plant compounds in fruits deteriorate over time, so purchasing the freshest fruit you can find will ensure you get all of its benefits. And because many fruits have thin, edible skins, opting for organic will help minimize your intake of the toxic pesticide residue that contaminates many conventionally grown varieties.

STRAWBERRIES

One of summer's treasures, juicy, fragrant strawberries make an excellent addition to your Paleo diet. Ancient Greeks and Romans wrote about the strawberry, acknowledging its health benefits and medicinal value, and today's science explains why strawberries qualify as a Paleo superfood. Chock-full of antioxidants and other nutrients, these low-sugar fruits satisfy your sweet tooth while supporting your immune system and helping reduce your risk of heart disease and other inflammation-related health problems. Just remember to keep your servings reasonable (I do well with about one serving of strawberries or other low-sugar fruit per day) and don't add any sugar—after a week of adopting a Paleo diet, you'll be amazed at how sweet strawberries taste to you without any kind of added sweetener.

HEART PROTECTOR

Heart disease is the leading cause of death in the United States, but these little heart-shaped fruits can reduce your risk of developing cardiovascular problems. Your heart and blood vessels need protection from the onslaught of oxidative and inflammatory damage they face every day. Strawberries contain a number of antioxidant plant compounds, including vitamin C, the red-purple pigment anthocyanins, and other flavonoids, that can defend against that damage.

Population studies show that people who consume a lot of vitamin C generally have a lower risk of heart disease, possibly because of its antioxidant effects. The plentiful antioxidants in strawberries directly improve several risk factors for cardiovascular disease as well, such as lowering high blood pressure and improving dyslipidemia (elevated levels of LDL ["bad"] cholesterol and triglycerides and too-low levels of HDL ["good"] cholesterol), according to a 2010 study in *Nutrition Research*. The same study found that strawberries help regulate blood sugar levels and control inflammation, two key features of the Paleo diet. It appears that the wide range of antioxidants in strawberries work together synergistically to provide these protective effects.

INFLAMMATION TAMER

Chronic inflammation can harm nearly every part of your body, increasing your risk of cardiovascular disease, obesity, diabetes, cancer, arthritis, vision loss, cognitive decline, and overall accelerated aging. But the antioxidants in strawberries help calm that harmful inflammation. For example, ½ cup (85 g) of sliced strawberries provides 16 percent of your daily requirement of manganese, an antioxidant that people typically get through eating whole grains. Because grains aren't a part of the Paleo diet, strawberries can help you get enough of this trace mineral that helps form one of the body's most powerful free radical scavengers and inflammation tamers: superoxide dismutase.

As with strawberries' heart benefits, all of the antioxidants work together to keep inflammation at bay. In one study, researchers triggered inflammation in a group of people by feeding them a high-carbohydrate, moderate-fat meal (much like the modern American diet). Consuming strawberries along with that meal significantly lowered the subjects' inflammatory response compared with a placebo. Strawberries' anti-inflammatory plant compounds may also lower the risk of developing age-related neurodegenerative diseases, noted a 2008 study in the *Journal of Agricultural and Food Chemistry*. Strawberries appear to protect against cancer as well, partly because their antioxidants can counteract, reduce, and repair damage resulting from oxidative stress and inflammation.

FUN FACT

Humans are among the few animals that can't synthesize vitamin C from glucose. And because vitamin C is a water-soluble nutrient, which means your body can't store it, it's important to consume enough vitamin C every day. Men should get at least 90 milligrams, and women should aim for at least 75 milligrams daily. Strawberries are a delicious way to help you reach your quota.

IMMUNITY BOOSTER

A ½ cup (85 g) of sliced strawberries provides 50 milligrams of vitamin C—about three-quarters of your daily requirement. Vitamin C acts as an antioxidant to mop up cell-damaging free radicals, and it actually regenerates other antioxidants in the body, such as vitamin E. It also helps your immune system work properly, reducing your risk of getting an infection, as well as limiting the severity and duration of any infections you do get. Your body maintains high levels of vitamin C in white blood cells called leukocytes, but when you experience stress or get an infection, your vitamin C levels plummet. Because your body can't store vitamin C, replenishing your levels by eating foods rich in this antioxidant (strawberries) will help keep your immune system functioning at its peak.

SHOPPING FOR STRAWBERRIES

Conventionally grown strawberries contain high levels of toxic pesticide residue, according to the Environmental Working Group, so buy organic whenever you can. If you find a local farm or patch where you can pick your own, be sure to ask about the growing practices. Strawberries peak from April through July—and buying them in season and locally really does make a difference in the flavor of these fragile fruits. Choose berries that are plump, shiny, deep red, free of mold, and still have their green caps. Store unwashed, uncut, and unhulled strawberries in the refrigerator for up to four days (remove any moldy or damaged strawberries first so they don't contaminate the rest).

STRAWBERRY AVOCADO SALSA WITH GRILLED CHICKEN

Strawberries have high levels of vitamin C, making them a natural immune booster, and avocados supply anti-inflammatory polyphenols and flavonoids. If you haven't tried the combination of these powerhouses together, this sweet and savory salsa will win you over.

FOR CHICKEN:

4 boneless, skinless chicken breasts

2 tablespoons (30 ml) extra-virgin olive oil, divided

1 teaspoon sea salt

½ teaspoon ground pepper

FOR STRAWBERRY AVOCADO SALSA:

1 cup (170 g) finely chopped strawberries

⅓ cup (50 g) peeled and finely cubed avocado

2 tablespoons (12 g) chopped fresh mint or basil

1 tablespoon (10 g) finely diced red onion

½ teaspoon lime zest

2 tablespoons (30 ml) lime juice

¼ teaspoon sea salt

¼ teaspoon freshly ground black pepper

To make the chicken: Preheat a grill to medium-high heat. Drizzle each chicken breast with ½ tablespoon (7.5 ml) olive oil and season with salt and pepper. Grill the chicken until cooked through, about 4 to 5 minutes per side. Let stand for 5 minutes.

To make the salsa: Add all the salsa ingredients to a medium bowl and gently toss to combine.

Serve immediately over the prepared chicken (or protein of choice).

MAKES 4 SERVINGS

TIP

This salsa also works well with sautéed fish or grilled pork tenderloin.

BLUEBERRIES

Blueberries may be a tiny fruit, but they offer mighty health benefits. Packed with free radical–quenching antioxidants, these gems land on many superfood lists, but they are of special value as part of the Paleo diet. In fact, as a low-sugar fruit that provides healthy carbohydrates to boost energy (especially important if you're living an active Paleo lifestyle), offers exceptional antioxidant content, and doesn't cause your blood sugar to spike, they're pretty much the ideal Paleo super fruit. Good things really do come in small packages!

ANTIOXIDANT POWERHOUSE

You're exposed to free radicals (unstable, highly reactive molecules formed during a process called oxidation, or oxygen metabolism) just about everywhere, from environmental factors such as cigarette smoke, air pollution, and ultraviolet light from the sun, to the ones that form naturally when your body converts food into energy. While your body can cope with a certain amount of free radicals, an overload can damage DNA, lipids, and cells in nearly every system of your body, which is why consuming antioxidants is so important to good health.

BLUEBERRY BONUS

Blueberries are a good addition to a dairy-free Paleo diet—besides all of their other benefits, 1 cup (145 g) of blueberries provides a surprising 36 percent of the bone-strengthening vitamin K you need daily.

One cup (145 g) of blueberries contains impressive amounts of potent antioxidants including vitamin C (24 percent of your daily requirement), the trace mineral manganese (25 percent of what you need daily), and the anthocyanins that give them their deep blue hue. They also contain smaller amounts of vitamin A, copper, zinc, and selenium, offering a wide spectrum of antioxidant protection. In fact, by some measures, blueberries contain more antioxidants than any other fruit! These antioxidants keep your immune system working properly, protect your cardiovascular system, reduce your risk of cancer, stave off cognitive decline (see below), quell harmful inflammation, and essentially slow down the aging process. Not bad for a simple bowl of berries!

BRAIN BOOSTER

Blueberries boast significant brain benefits, from improving cognitive function and memory to delaying the neurological decline that occurs with aging. Oxidative damage is particularly detrimental to the brain because your body can't readily replace damaged neurons. But the anthocyanins in blueberries can cross the blood-brain barrier, directly protecting your brain cells and structures against free radical attacks.

So far, most of the research on blueberries has examined the effects of blueberry extracts or isolated antioxidants in animals or in the lab, but early studies in humans are encouraging. For example, in one study that followed more than 16,000 women, researchers noted that the women who ate the most blueberries and strawberries delayed memory decline by up to two and a half years. Evidence suggests that the flavonoids in blueberries influence memory and learning processes in the hippocampus, where spatial learning occurs.

BLOOD SUGAR STABILIZER

Blueberries contain 14.6 grams of naturally occurring sugars per cup (145 g), but they also offer nearly 4 grams of fiber, which helps you achieve the Paleo goal of stable blood sugar. That explains why even though blueberries have a moderately high glycemic index of 40 to 53 (glycemic index is a measure of how foods impact blood sugar compared with pure glucose), they have a glycemic load value of just 6 (glycemic load takes into account the percentage of the food that is carbohydrate; a value of less than 10 is considered low).

Blueberries contain both soluble and insoluble fiber, and each influences blood sugar in different ways. Soluble fiber binds with water in your digestive tract to form a gel that slows digestion so you don't absorb as much starch or sugar through your stomach and intestine, and it promotes a slower, more controlled release of glucose into your blood. Interestingly, though, research indicates that *insoluble* fiber matters more in reducing your risk of type 2 diabetes, possibly by helping to improve insulin sensitivity. Blueberries' insoluble fiber, which helps speed the passage of food and waste products through your digestive tract, is found in their skins.

BUYING THE BEST BLUEBERRIES

The blueberry season extends from May through October, but these berries are at their best in July (designated National Blueberry Month in the United States). As always, opt for organic whenever you can—not only will you reduce your exposure to toxic pesticide residues, but organic blueberries may also have more antioxidant capacity than conventionally grown blueberries, according to a 2008 study in the *Journal of Agricultural and Food Chemistry*.

Choose blueberries that are firm and uniformly colored, and store them unwashed in the refrigerator for up to four days. (Discard any berries that are moldy or crushed so they don't contaminate the rest.) Before using, wash them gently and remove any stem pieces that are still attached to the berries. You'll get the most antioxidant benefit by eating your blueberries raw—heating them destroys some of their anthocyanins (but you can freeze them for several months without affecting their antioxidant levels, which is good news when you have a blueberry craving in January!).

BLUEBERRY WAFFLES

With a hint of spice and an abundance of antioxidant-rich blueberries, these waffles are one of my family's favorite Sunday morning breakfast treats. No waffle maker? No problem. This recipe can easily be made into pancakes for another breakfast option.

2 eggs

½ cup plus 2 tablespoons (150 ml) coconut milk

1 tablespoon (15 ml) vanilla extract

1 large ripe banana, mashed (about ½ cup [115 g])

½ tablespoon maple syrup

1 tablespoon (14 g) coconut oil, melted

1¼ cups (150 g) almond flour

¼ teaspoon sea salt

½ teaspoon baking soda

1 teaspoon ground cinnamon

1 tablespoon (8 g) coconut flour

½ cup (75 g) fresh blueberries, plus more for topping

Shredded coconut or banana slices, for topping (optional)

In a medium bowl, whisk together the eggs, coconut milk, vanilla extract, banana, maple syrup, and coconut oil until smooth.

In a separate bowl combine the almond flour, salt, baking soda, cinnamon, and coconut flour. Add the dry ingredients to the wet ingredients and mix until combined. Gently fold in the blueberries.

Preheat and grease your waffle iron. Pour one-quarter of the batter into the waffle iron and cook until golden brown (or cook according to your waffle iron's instructions).

Top the waffles with additional blueberries, shredded coconut, or banana slices, if desired, and serve.

MAKES 4 LARGE WAFFLES

TIDBIT:

You can also transform this recipe into muffins. Preheat your oven to 350°F (180°C, or gas mark 4). Line a 12-cup muffin pan with liners. Fill cups with batter and bake 20 to 25 minutes or until golden.

BLACKBERRIES

These low-sugar fruits are not actually berries at all—they're considered an aggregate, with several individual seeded fruits, or drupelets, attached to a single core. The resulting high percentage of skin and seeds makes blackberries an incredibly nutrient- and antioxidant-rich fruit, and a true Paleo superfood. Blackberries originated more than 30 million years ago in Asia, Europe, and North and South America, and they still grow all over the world (although it's a lot easier to gather them these days, thanks to the introduction of thornless varieties in the past few centuries). Their healthy carbohydrates provide long-lasting energy that makes blackberries a great pre- or post-workout snack, and their high fiber content helps make up for some of the fiber you lose by not consuming whole grains or legumes on the Paleo diet.

BLACKBERRY TRIVIA

There are more than 1,000 known species of blackberries today, and in some countries (such as Australia) they grow so prolifically that they're considered a weed. The Greeks used blackberries to treat gout, Egyptians used their dark juice as a hair dye, and the thorny bushes were frequently planted to keep out intruders.

CANCER PREVENTER

Blackberries contain an astonishing array of antioxidants, in very high concentrations. In addition to large amounts of vitamin C (50 percent of your daily requirement in 1 cup [145 g]) and manganese (nearly half of what you need daily), blackberries contain the reddish purple anthocyanins and a laundry list of other flavonoids. These antioxidants work together to help counteract, reduce, and repair damage from inflammation and free radicals in your cells and DNA that can lead to cancer. Lab and animal studies show specific anticancer effects for many of blackberries' flavonoids—for example, ellagic acid appears to reduce the effect of estrogen in breast cancer cell growth, causes cancer cells to die, and helps your liver break down and remove carcinogens from your blood—but more research is needed to see whether these results translate to humans.

The fiber in blackberries may also help reduce your risk of cancer. For decades, scientists have examined the link between fiber intake and colorectal cancer and possibly breast cancer. Study results have been mixed, but recent evidence indicates that fiber from fruits and vegetables (as opposed to grains) might be more helpful. That's good news for our grain-free Paleo lifestyles.

HEART HELPER

One cup (145 g) of blackberries provides a seriously impressive 8 grams of fiber (more than a third of what women need daily, and more than 20 percent of what men should get). In addition to promoting healthy digestion and possibly reducing your cancer risk, the fiber in blackberries can reduce your risk of heart disease. Soluble fiber binds to bile acids in your digestive tract, helping to lower your LDL ("bad") cholesterol and total cholesterol levels. Dietary fiber can also reduce circulating levels of C-reactive protein, a marker for inflammation that's linked to risk of cardiovascular disease. All that adds up to significant heart protection—researchers in the Netherlands followed more than 1,300 men for forty years and found that for every additional 10 grams of fiber they consumed per day, they reduced their risk of dying from heart disease by 17 percent!

Blackberries also provide a good amount of heart-protecting potassium (233 milligrams per cup [145 g]). This mineral helps your heart beat normally, lowers blood pressure, and reduces your overall risk of dying from cardiovascular disease. And, of course, there are all those antioxidants that work to calm inflammation and fend off free radical damage to blood vessels and LDL cholesterol (which builds up as plaque in your arteries and can lead to a heart attack or stroke). In particular, studies suggest that vitamin C may keep your arteries flexible and slow down the progression of atherosclerosis (hardening of the arteries).

KEEPING BLACKBERRIES AT THEIR BEST

Blackberries start blooming in mid-June, but they usually don't ripen until mid-July through mid-September. Unripe blackberries are hard and tart, and they won't ripen once they've been picked, so it pays to be patient. (For this reason, skip berries that still have their hulls attached—a sign they were picked too early.) Look for blackberries that have a deep, rich color and are plump. As with the other berries in this chapter, buy local and organic blackberries whenever possible for the freshest, best-tasting berries with the lowest amount of toxic pesticide residue.

Don't wash blackberries until you're ready to use them—the moisture will cause them to mold. Remove any damaged or decaying berries before placing them in a single layer on a plate; cover loosely and store them in the refrigerator. Blackberries will keep for two to three days.

BLACKBERRY-GLAZED SALMON

This dish is wonderful during the late spring and summer months when blackberries are at their ripest and can be found at your local market in abundance. I like to serve this dish with steamed asparagus or over a nice spinach salad.

FOR SALMON:

Zest of 1 lemon

1 tablespoon (1.7 g) fresh rosemary, chopped

1 clove garlic, minced

¼ teaspoon sea salt

¼ teaspoon freshly ground black pepper

2 (6- to 8-ounce, or 168 to 224 g) wild-caught salmon fillets

FOR GLAZE:

½ cup (75 g) fresh blackberries, plus additional for garnish, if desired

¼ cup (60 ml) balsamic vinegar

½ teaspoon fresh rosemary, minced

To make the salmon: In a small bowl, combine the lemon zest, rosemary, garlic, sea salt, and pepper and mix together. Rub the lemon-herb mixture on the salmon fillets. Place on a plate, cover with plastic wrap, and refrigerate for at least 3 hours or (even better) overnight.

Remove the salmon from the refrigerator and scrape the lemon-herb mixture off the salmon. Heat a nonstick skillet over medium-high heat. When the skillet is hot, add the salmon fillets flesh side down, and cook until a nice golden crust forms, about 4 to 5 minutes. Flip the fillets and continue cooking until the skin becomes nice and crispy, about 3 to 4 minutes.

To make the glaze: While the fish is cooking, mash the blackberries in a small bowl with the back of a spoon. Combine the blackberry mash, vinegar, and rosemary in a small frying pan. Place it over medium heat and stir occasionally. Allow the liquid to reduce by about half, about 3 to 5 minutes. It will thicken and become syrupy. Stir in a few additional whole blackberries, if desired.

Spoon the glaze over the top of the salmon and serve.

MAKES 2 SERVINGS

RASPBERRIES

With only 5 grams of naturally occurring sugars and a remarkable 8 grams of fiber per cup (145 g), sweet-tart raspberries are a delicious and healthy summer treat. Like blackberries, raspberries are considered aggregate fruits rather than true berries. Both bramble fruits are actually a collection of smaller seed fruits called drupelets that grow on canes. Raspberries are smaller and more delicate, however, and they have a hollow core when picked. Wild raspberries have been around since the Paleolithic era—they were likely a major carbohydrate source for hunter-gatherer societies—and wild varieties are still popular even with the profusion of cultivated raspberries available today.

FREE RADICAL NEUTRALIZER

Like other berries, raspberries earn their superfood status because of their sky-high antioxidant levels, and studies show that both wild and cultivated raspberries boast similar levels of antioxidant plant compounds. The major antioxidant phytochemicals in raspberries are anthocyanins (the red-purple pigment that gives raspberries their gem-like hue) and ellagitannins (a complex plant polyphenol that contributes to raspberries' flavor), but they also provide more than half of the vitamin C you should aim for daily and 41 percent of your daily requirement of the antioxidant trace mineral manganese, plus smaller amounts of other flavonoids. This wide spectrum of antioxidants provides powerful protection against a range of harmful free radicals that damage cells and contribute to aging, inflammation, cancer, heart disease, age-related vision problems, and neurodegenerative diseases.

Thanks to their inflammation-calming abilities, anthocyanins and ellagitannins might protect cartilage and reduce the onset and severity of arthritis, suggests a 2011 animal study in the *Journal of Agricultural and Food Chemistry*. Early research shows that ellagic acid, a derivative of ellagitannins, may also calm the free radical–induced inflammation and intestinal damage of Crohn's disease. And ellagitannins show particular promise in preventing cancer. For example, a 2007 study in the journal *Phytochemistry* found that ellagitannins from raspberry extracts were better than anthocyanins at stopping cervical cancer cells from multiplying. Other research shows that breakdown products of ellagitannins inhibit prostate cancer cell growth. Additional research will show whether these promising results translate to humans.

A NATURAL BEAUTY

Raspberries are not just good for eating—they're good as a topical skin treatment as well! Raspberry seed oil contains skin-nourishing vitamin E and omega-3 fatty acids, and it has a natural sun protection factor (SPF) of 25 to 50, which has led cosmetics manufacturers to investigate using it in skin care products.

OBESITY FIGHTER

No grains or legumes? No worries! You don't need them when you've got fiber-rich raspberries on hand. Their impressive amount of fiber helps regulate blood sugar levels and insulin sensitivity, which makes it easier for you to stay at a healthy weight and reduces your risk of type 2 diabetes. They also provide small amounts of many B vitamins, which help your body properly metabolize carbohydrates, protein, and fats. But even beyond these nutrients, raspberries supply other substances that might prove helpful for weight control. Researchers have begun investigating two in particular: raspberry ketones (rheosmin, an aromatic compound) and a type of flavonoid called tiliroside.

Animal studies suggest that raspberry ketones change the way your body metabolizes fats, which could help prevent or reduce obesity and fatty liver. Tiliroside prevented weight gain and fat accumulation in normal mice and helped obese mice better regulate their blood sugar and lower their cholesterol levels, according to a pair of Japanese studies. Although it's too early to tell whether these compounds will work the same way in humans, raspberries' other benefits are more than enough reason to make them a regular part of your Paleo diet.

SHOPPING FOR RASPBERRIES

Of the more than 200 species of raspberries available on five continents, bright red are the most popular—followed closely by black raspberries—but you can also find gold, purple, and white raspberries. In the United States, raspberries are at their best from mid-summer through early fall. As always, go for organic whenever possible (or at least ask the vendor about their growing practices) to reduce your exposure to toxic pesticide residue. Choose raspberries that are firm, plump, and deeply colored, and remove any that are mushy or moldy before storing in the refrigerator. (Not only does keeping them refrigerated prevent them from spoiling so quickly, but it also preserves their antioxidant levels better than leaving them at room temperature.)

You can keep raspberries in their original container as long as they're not packed too tightly, but they might last a little longer spread out in a single layer on a plate or in a dish. Eat these delicate, highly perishable fruits within a day or two of purchasing. Raspberries tend to be expensive because they're soft and bruise easily, which makes them difficult to pick and ship. Buying local (or picking your own) may help keep costs down.

Research shows that freezing doesn't affect the antioxidant capacity or levels of phytochemicals in raspberries, so feel free to extend raspberries' short growing season by enjoying frozen berries all year long. To freeze your own, rinse raspberries gently and pat dry. Spread in a single layer on a baking sheet or plate and put in the freezer. Once frozen, transfer them to an airtight container and store in the freezer for up to one year.

FOUR BERRY MINT SALAD WITH COCONUT WHIPPED CREAM

Raspberries, strawberries, blackberries, and blueberries at their peak in the summer make for the most spectacular "sweet" treat. A few sprigs of mint give this salad a refreshing twist.

FOR SALAD:

1 cup (145 g) raspberries

1 cup (170 g) sliced strawberries

1 cup (145 g) blueberries

1 cup (145 g) blackberries

2 tablespoons (12 g) fresh mint, chopped, plus more for garnish

½ tablespoon fresh lemon juice

FOR COCONUT WHIPPED CREAM:

2 cans (13½-ounce, or 378 g) full-fat coconut milk

1 tablespoon (15 ml) maple syrup

1 teaspoon vanilla extract

To make the salad: Combine all the berries in a medium bowl. Add the fresh mint and lemon juice and gently toss to combine.

To make the whipped cream: Place the canned coconut milk in the refrigerator overnight. Open the can without shaking or turning it upside down. Carefully spoon out the top layer of thick coconut cream and add to the bowl of a stand mixer. Leave the white liquid part at the bottom in the can and save for other uses.

Add the maple syrup and vanilla extract to the coconut cream. Whip the coconut mixture with the whisk attachment starting on low and moving to a higher speed as it becomes creamy. Mix for about 5 minutes, or until you have thick whipped peaks.

Transfer the berry salad to a serving bowl and top with the coconut whipped cream. Top with additional mint or a berry if desired, and serve immediately.

MAKES 4 SERVINGS

CHERRIES

Cherries have a long history as a favored fruit—some evidence suggests the ancient Romans may have brought certain varieties of cherries to Britain when they occupied the country in the first century CE. Today, cherries grow all over the world, from the United States to Italy and Japan. Although cherries contain more natural sugars than low-sugar fruits like berries, their fiber ensures that those sugars are digested slowly and released gradually into your bloodstream. That makes them a perfect Paleo-friendly source of energy-boosting carbohydrates. Cherries also supply good amounts of vitamin C, potassium, and the antioxidant anthocyanins that give them their gorgeous ruby-red color and provide many of cherries' health benefits.

NATURE'S PAIN RELIEVER

The next time you're in pain, try snacking on cherries instead of popping a pill. The anthocyanins and other antioxidant plant compounds in cherries inhibit enzymes called cyclooxygenase-1 and -2 (COX-1 and -2), which are the targets of anti-inflammatory medicines such as aspirin and popular arthritis drugs such as Celebrex. In fact, several lab studies from Michigan State University researchers indicate that cherry extracts can inhibit between 80 and 95 percent of COX-1 and COX-2 enzymes (depending on the variety), which makes them as effective as the over-the-counter pain relievers ibuprofen and naproxen.

Research in humans is also encouraging. Cherries inhibit inflammation in a number of ways, according to a 2013 study in the *Journal of Nutrition*. In the study, researchers followed eighteen men and women who ate two servings of Bing cherries every day for twenty-eight days. Blood samples confirmed that the cherries reduced nine different markers of inflammation associated with inflammatory diseases. An earlier study found that, along with reducing measures of inflammation such as C-reactive protein and nitric oxide, Bing cherries lower blood levels of a substance called urate that causes gout (an extremely painful type of arthritis that frequently affects the big toe joints).

Tart cherries can also reduce inflammation, and they may be especially useful for reducing muscle pain and damage after strenuous exercise—good news for people who've adopted an active Paleo lifestyle. Long-distance runners who drank tart cherry juice for a week prior to and during a race rated their pain significantly less than those who drank a placebo cherry drink, according to a 2010 study in the *Journal of the International Society of Sports Nutrition*. A similar study that followed marathon runners found that not only were measures of inflammation notice-ably lower in runners who drank cherry juice for five days prerace and two days afterward, but their muscle strength also recovered more quickly and the levels of antioxidants in their blood increased by 10 percent compared with runners given the placebo drink.

HEART HELPER

Both sweet and tart cherries calm heart-harming inflammation, including reducing levels of C-reactive protein that indicates heart disease risk. In fact, in the *Journal of Nutrition* study of people who ate cherries for twenty-eight days, the fruits reduced levels of C-reactive protein by 20 percent. But cherries boast other heart benefits as well, including more than 300 milligrams of potassium per cup (155 g). Potassium helps lower your blood pressure, offsetting the effects of sodium. That fits right in with the contemporary Paleolithic diet, which contains 12.5 times as much potassium as sodium, according to a 2002 review in the *Journal of the American Nutraceutical Association*.

Cherries also contain an antioxidant flavonoid called quercetin that protects your heart in multiple ways. Lab and animal studies show that quercetin can lower high blood pressure, lower levels of LDL ("bad") cholesterol, and reduce the risk of atherosclerosis (plaque buildup in arteries that can lead to heart attack and stroke).

CHOOSING CHERRIES

Fresh cherries are in season from May through August. Sweet cherries, such as Bing or Rainier, are better for snacking, but you can use either sweet or tart varieties for cooking. Look for large, plump, firm cherries with unblemished, glossy skin. If possible, buy cherries with fresh-looking green stems still attached, which indicates freshness and will help the cherries last longer. In general, a deeper red color indicates sweeter cherries (yellow-and-red Rainier cherries excepted), but you can ask if the seller will let you taste the cherries before purchasing to ensure that you'll like the batch you're about to buy.

EAT CHERRIES FOR A BETTER NIGHT'S SLEEP

If you need a little help falling (or staying) asleep, try eating cherries before bed—tart cherries contain melatonin, a hormone your body produces that helps set your circadian rhythms and makes you sleepy. After consuming tart Montmorency cherry juice for a week, a group of volunteers reported spending more time in bed, more total sleep time, and better sleep efficiency, according to a 2012 study in the *European Journal of Nutrition*.

Cherries are highly perishable, so you'll want to eat them within a day or two of purchasing. To extend their life, don't wash them until you're ready to eat them, leave the stems on, and store in a bowl or an open bag in the refrigerator. Cherries freeze well and will keep, frozen, for up to a year. To freeze cherries, rinse them well and thoroughly pat dry. Spread in a single layer on a baking sheet or plate with a rim, freeze overnight, and transfer to an airtight container.

To pit cherries, you can either use a specially designed pitting tool—which also works well for olives—or cut the cherry in half and remove the pit with the knife tip. If you're going to cook the cherries (or if you don't care if they look nice), you can also smash the cherry with the flat of a chef's knife and pick out the pit.

GRILLED CHICKEN WITH CHERRIES AND WATERCRESS

Cherries take center stage in this refreshing dish. This stone fruit makes a brief appearance from June until August, making this the ultimate summertime meal. As a bonus, the watercress in this recipe provides bone-strengthening potassium and vitamin K.

1 clove garlic, minced

1 teaspoon apple cider vinegar

1 tablespoon (2.5 g) fresh basil, chopped

2 tablespoons (30 ml) extra-virgin olive oil, divided

2 halves (about 1 pound, or 454 g) boneless, skinless chicken breast

Coarse salt and freshly ground black pepper

8 ounces (224 g) sweet cherries, pitted and halved

1 cup (40 g) watercress

Combine the garlic, vinegar, basil, and 1 tablespoon (15 ml) of the oil and set aside.

Preheat a grill to medium-high. Drizzle the remaining 1 tablespoon (15 ml) oil over the chicken and season with salt and pepper. Grill the chicken until cooked through, 4 to 5 minutes per side. Let stand for 5 minutes.

Toss the garlic mixture, cherries, and watercress in a small bowl and season with salt and pepper. Serve on top of grilled chicken.

MAKES 2 SERVINGS

TIDBIT:
Check out the tips on page 129 for help in pitting cherries.

GRAPEFRUIT

Grapefruits are a rather recent addition to the citrus fruit family. Discovered in Barbados in the eighteenth century, grapefruit is an accidental hybrid between the pummelo and the orange that likely gets its name because it grows in grape-like bunches. The flesh can range from pale yellow to ruby red, and although the color doesn't affect the flavor, it does reflect the antioxidant content (see below). Packed with antioxidants and fiber (plus good amounts of blood pressure–lowering potassium and energy-producing B vitamins) that can help protect you against a host of modern ailments, grapefruit is a superfood to include in a contemporary Paleo diet.

ANTIOXIDANT SUPERSTAR

Grapefruits are practically bursting with vitamin C—1 cup (145 g) of grapefruit sections provides 72 milligrams, or 120 percent of your recommended daily intake. Vitamin C holds a special place in the antioxidant world because not only does it scavenge cell-destroying free radicals on its own, but it also regenerates other antioxidants (such as vitamin E) so they can keep working. Research suggests that vitamin C might help prevent or delay diseases caused by oxidative stress, such as cardiovascular disease and certain cancers. And it helps keep your immune system functioning at its best.

Grapefruit also supplies more than half of the vitamin A you need every day in the form of beta-carotene. Studies have shown that beta-carotene and vitamin A have special benefit for your eyes, including protecting them from age-related macular degeneration and cataracts. And getting these antioxidants from food appears far more effective than taking supplements. For example, a high dietary intake of beta-carotene and vitamin C, along with vitamin E and zinc, may substantially reduce your risk of age-related macular degeneration, according to a 2005 study in the *Journal of the American Medical Association*.

But that's not all. Red and pink grapefruits get their color from lycopene (the same antioxidant in tomatoes). Population studies suggest that because of its strength as a free radical fighter, lycopene might reduce the risk of certain cancers, especially prostate, lung, and stomach cancer. Your body absorbs lycopene better from cooked grapefruit eaten with a little Paleo-friendly fat, so in addition to enjoying grapefruit prepared according to the following recipe, give broiled grapefruit a try and serve it with a handful of almonds or a drizzle of coconut oil.

TIP:

If your grapefruit is bitter, a sprinkle of salt will make it taste sweeter.

BLOOD SUGAR BALANCER

One cup (145 g) of grapefruit sections contains 16 grams of natural sugars, but it also has 4 grams of dietary fiber to slow their absorption and encourage a steady, long-lasting release of those sugars into your bloodstream. And that fiber is especially important on the grain- and legume-free Paleo diet. As a source of healthful carbohydrates with a glycemic load of only 7 (glycemic load is a measure of the effect of a food on your blood sugar; anything less than 10 is considered low), grapefruit is a great Paleo fruit option.

Grapefruit also has a modest effect on your insulin levels, helping prevent blood sugar swings that deplete you of energy and trigger cravings, and possibly reducing your risk of blood sugar disorders such as diabetes. A group of volunteers who ate half a grapefruit before meals had lower insulin levels two hours after they ate than those who took a placebo capsule, according to a 2006 study in the *Journal of Medicinal Food*. Lab research also shows that a flavonoid in grapefruit called naringenin helps insulin work more effectively by increasing your muscles' ability to absorb and use glucose, found a 2010 study in the journal *Biochemical and Biophysical Research Communications*.

FINDING GREAT GRAPEFRUITS

Grapefruit season lasts from October through May, but you can find the fruit in grocery stores year-round. Seedless varieties are easier to prepare and eat, but regardless of what kind you choose, look for grapefruits with thin, smooth skin that feel heavy for their size and stay firm when squeezed. Grapefruits will last about one week at room temperature or two to three weeks refrigerated (let refrigerated grapefruits come to room temperature before eating for the juiciest fruit). You can peel and section a grapefruit with your hands, but for a nicer presentation, use a sharp knife to cut off the top and bottom. Then cut away the peel and white pith and slice along the membranes between segments.

GRAPEFRUIT AND DRUG INTERACTIONS

Grapefruit (and grapefruit juice) can interact dangerously with a long list of commonly prescribed medications, and it's not always enough to simply consume grapefruit at a different time than you take your medications. The fruit interferes with enzymes that break down the drugs in your digestive system so your body can use them, which means the drugs may stay in your system for too long, or not long enough, or have their absorption increased to risky levels. Be sure to ask your doctor or pharmacist whether this is an issue with any of the medications you take.

But also keep in mind that following a Paleo lifestyle can help you improve or eliminate some of the underlying conditions that require those drugs, such as high blood pressure, high cholesterol, and diabetes. As your health improves, ask your doctor whether you can reduce your dosages or at what point you might be able to stop taking the medication altogether (never stop taking a prescribed drug without your doctor's okay). Then you can eat all the grapefruit you want!

GRAPEFRUIT-AVOCADO SALAD CUPS

These salad cups make a refreshing side dish for a hot summer meal of grilled fish or chicken. The avocado in this recipe acts as a nutrient booster—its healthy fats help your body absorb the antioxidant lycopene in the grapefruit.

¼ cup (60 ml) plus 2 teaspoons lemon juice, divided (about 2 to 3 large lemons)

2 avocados, halved lengthwise, pitted

2 red grapefruits

½ teaspoon coarse salt

2 tablespoons (5 g) chopped fresh basil, plus more for garnish

Freshly ground pepper

¼ cup (60 ml) olive oil

Lime wedges, for serving

Brush 2 teaspoons of the lemon juice over the flesh of the avocados to keep them from turning brown; set aside.

Remove the peel and pith from the grapefruits using a sharp paring knife. Working over a medium bowl to catch the juice, carefully carve out segments from between the membranes. Transfer the grapefruit segments to a small bowl; set aside. Reserve the juice in the bowl.

Add the remaining ¼ cup (60 ml) lemon juice, salt, and basil to the grapefruit juice; season with pepper. Whisk in the oil in a slow, steady stream. Add the grapefruit sections; toss gently just to coat.

Place each avocado half on a plate. Top with the grapefruit mixture, dividing evenly. Garnish with additional basil and serve with lime wedges.

MAKES 4 SERVINGS

TIP:

To remove the pit of an avocado without damaging the flesh, halve the avocado lengthwise, then gently tap the sharp edge of a large knife into the pit. Twist the knife, holding on to the avocado firmly, and the pit should come out easily.

FIGS

Mentioned in the Bible and other ancient writings, figs have a long and storied history. Possibly more than 780,000 years of history, according to archaeological evidence from northern Israel. And although today's figs are likely bigger and sweeter than those early fruits, our ancestors certainly enjoyed them—and we should, too.

Typical Western diets that rely on fake energy sources such as caffeine and refined sugar to keep you going eventually leave you feeling depleted, with barely enough oomph to get through the day, much less be as physically active as you should. But Paleo superfoods such as figs provide you with real energy from high-quality carbohydrates. Figs boast the minerals potassium, magnesium, iron, and calcium that give you energy and also help keep your bones strong. And like all of the Paleo super fruits, figs contain a wealth of antioxidants. There are hundreds of varieties of figs, ranging in color from white to almost black. Although you might be most familiar with dried figs, fresh figs are delicious as well, and it's the fresh ones that we'll talk about here.

FUEL YOUR WORKOUTS

Figs are lusciously sweet, which reflects their slightly higher natural sugar content, but they also provide an abundance of fiber to slow the release of those sugars in your bloodstream so you get a steady supply of energy. Three medium figs contain 4.5 grams of fiber, a significant contribution to the 25 grams a day women need and 38 grams men should aim for daily, especially in the absence of grains and legumes.

Those same three medium figs provide 350 milligrams of potassium, or about 7 percent of your daily recommended intake. Potassium plays an essential role in muscle contraction and nerve communication, helping your heart beat regularly and your skeletal muscles power through a tough workout. Potassium also helps keep your blood pressure low so your heart can pump oxygen-rich blood through your body much more efficiently. That allows you to work out harder without feeling like you're expending more effort—perfect for an active Paleo lifestyle.

Figs are also a good source of magnesium, which is critical for every organ in your body, and especially your heart and muscles. Like potassium, magnesium supports muscle and nerve function, keeping your heart rhythm steady, and it lowers blood pressure. Magnesium also keeps your energy levels up by helping your body use glucose properly and by producing a substance called adenosine triphosphate (ATP), your body's primary energy source.

Along with magnesium, the iron in figs helps produce ATP. And iron keeps you revved by bringing energizing oxygen to every cell in your body. The type of iron figs contain, called non-heme iron, gets absorbed better when you consume it with vitamin C. Although figs do contain a little vitamin C themselves, you can boost the iron absorption by eating figs along with another food rich in vitamin C.

BOOST YOUR BONES

If you're concerned about getting enough calcium now that you've cut out dairy as part of the Paleo diet, try snacking on figs. These delicious fruits are a surprisingly good source of calcium, with three medium figs supplying about 6 percent of your daily requirement. (To maximize your calcium absorption, avoid eating figs at the same time as foods high in oxalic or phytic acid, such as spinach and collard greens, and nuts and seeds.) But calcium isn't the only mineral critical for bone health. The potassium in figs also keeps your bones strong, decreasing your risk of osteoporosis. And your bones contain about half of all your body's magnesium. This multitasking mineral also helps regulate calcium levels in your body.

EAT MORE ANTIOXIDANTS

Figs supply a stellar amount of antioxidants that fight cell-damaging free radicals, protecting you against oxidative damage that can lead to heart disease, cancer, and all kinds of inflammation-related diseases. While all figs contain antioxidant polyphenols, flavonoids, and anthocyanins, darker-colored varieties provide the highest overall antioxidant levels, with the skin contributing most of those compounds. In a comparison of the antioxidant content of six different types of figs ranging in color from black to red, yellow, and green, black Mission figs came out on top, according to a 2006 study in the *Journal of Agricultural and Food Chemistry*.

DRIED FIGS AND SULFITES

Dried figs (and other dried fruits) are frequently treated with sulfur dioxide gas or sulfites as a preservative. Approximately one in 100 people are sensitive to sulfites (especially people with asthma) and can experience adverse reactions after consuming them. The U.S. Department of Agriculture prohibits the use of sulfites in foods labeled organic, so opt for organic dried figs if you're concerned about sulfite exposure.

FIND FANTASTIC FIGS

Look for fresh figs at your market from June to early fall. Choose deeply colored figs that are plump and tender but not mushy or bruised. Check that the skin is clean, dry, smooth, and unbroken. And give them a sniff—fresh figs should smell mildly sweet, but a sour smell means they may be past their prime. These highly perishable fruits spoil quickly (which is why dried figs are more readily available), so store them in a plastic bag in the coldest part of your refrigerator and eat them within two days of purchasing. Their skin is edible, so they just need a quick rinse and then they're ready to enjoy!

FRESH FIG VANILLA HONEY COMPOTE

The flavors of cinnamon and vanilla give this compote a warm edge, while the sweetness of the fig makes it shine. Pair this compote with homemade Paleo biscuits, use as a topping for the Pumpkin Pancakes with Toasted Pecans (page 92) in place of sugary syrups, or use as a sweet dipping sauce for meats (such as lamb, pork, or chicken).

1½ cups (225 g) fresh figs, stems trimmed and cut into quarters

2 tablespoons (40 g) honey

½ cup (120 ml) water

1 teaspoon ground cinnamon

½ teaspoon vanilla extract

1 tablespoon (14 g) coconut oil

Place the figs, honey, water, cinnamon, and vanilla extract in a small saucepan over low heat. Stir occasionally and cook for 30 minutes. Remove from the heat and stir in the coconut oil while the mixture is still warm.

Using a food processor, process until the mixture is smooth and has reached a spread-like consistency.

Serve immediately or store in an airtight container in the refrigerator for up to 2 weeks.

MAKES ¾ CUP (240 G)

APPLES

Apples are one of the most popular fruits in all of the world's temperate regions. Scientists have determined that the cultivated apples we eat today originated from wild apples in central Asia about 4,000 years ago, with other wild species along the Silk Route running from Asia to Western Europe possibly contributing as well. With a dizzying number of varieties to choose from, this iconic fruit serves up good amounts of fiber and potassium, plus vitamin C and other antioxidants. Add that to their long history and the fact that apples supply slow-burning carbohydrates that provide a steady flow of energy, and you have one outstanding Paleo superfood.

CARE FOR YOUR HEART

An apple a day keeps the cardiologist away! The fiber, potassium, and antioxidants in apples help protect your heart and blood vessels in many ways. If you're concerned that giving up grains and legumes on the Paleo diet means you won't get enough fiber, apples will put that fear to rest. One large apple (3¼ inches [8.3 cm] in diameter) has a stellar 5.4 grams of fiber, or 22 percent of what women need daily and 14 percent of what men should get. That fiber can lower your cholesterol—especially LDL ("bad") cholesterol—and reduce high blood pressure. Research also shows that diets high in fiber can help regulate your blood sugar, help you stay at a healthy weight, and calm inflammation. All those protective mechanisms add up, to the point where every additional 10 grams of fiber you consume per day lowers your risk of dying from heart disease by 17 percent. Additionally, the higher your fiber intake, the lower your risk of first-time stroke, according to a 2013 study in the journal *Stroke*.

Potassium plays a role in preventing heart disease as well. Getting enough potassium in your diet helps your heart keep a steady rhythm and lowers high blood pressure. And increasing your intake of this mineral can reduce your chance of dying from heart disease, notes a 2008 review in the journal *Physiologia Plantarum*. The researchers also pointed out that in most developed countries, humans consume only about one-third the potassium we used to before the introduction of processed foods, and that the best way to boost your intake is to eat more fruits and vegetables.

JOHNNY APPLESEED

The legendary figure Johnny Appleseed, famous for spreading apple seeds all over the United States, is actually a real person! Born in Massachusetts in 1775, Jonathan Chapman was a professional nurseryman who earned his nickname because he walked across 100,000 square miles of prairie and wilderness in the Midwest, planting orchards and individual apple trees as he traveled.

Apples contain a variety of antioxidants, many of which are found in the brightly pigmented skin. In addition to supplying 17 percent of your recommended daily intake of heart-protective vitamin C, apples provide polyphenols such as anthocyanins, quercetin, and catechins. Lab studies show that the antioxidants in apples fight free radicals to decrease lipid oxidation (a primary risk factor for cardiovascular problems), lower cholesterol, and calm heart-harming inflammation.

A BUSHEL OF APPLES

Markets in the United States sell upwards of 100 apple varieties, each with a distinct combination of flavor, color, texture, and phytochemicals. Some of the most popular include:

BRAEBURN: Rich, sweet-tart, and almost spicy in flavor. Their skin color ranges from orange to red over a yellow background. Aromatic, juicy, and crisp, Braeburns are great for snacking and Paleo baking.

FUJI: Sweet, juicy, and crisp, Fujis are good snacking apples, but they also hold up well to baking.

GALA: Rosy red skin. Firm and crisp, Gala apples are great eaten out of hand or used in dishes to add slight sweetness.

GOLDEN DELICIOUS: Yellow to yellow-green skin. With a mildly sweet flavor and flesh that is juicy, resists browning, and provides a great crunch, they make great all-purpose apples but do lose some of their flavor when cooked.

GRANNY SMITH: Crisp and juicy, with bright green skin and sweetly tart flesh, this versatile apple is excellent for both snacking and cooking.

HONEYCRISP: Bright red and pale green skin with crisp, juicy flesh. Has a slightly tart flavor that makes it great for eating and for cooking.

McINTOSH: Red skin tinged with green. This tart-sweet apple is all-purpose but its tender flesh doesn't hold up to lengthy cooking.

RED DELICIOUS: Large apples with brilliant red skins. They have an elongated shape with five distinctive knobs at the base. Sweet, simple, and best for eating out of hand.

APPLE PICKING

Although you can readily find apples in the grocery store year-round, it's especially fun to follow in our ancestors' footsteps and pick your own at an orchard. Peak apple season in the northern hemisphere begins at the end of summer and runs through early winter. Apples available the rest of the year are generally imported from the southern hemisphere or brought out of cold storage, which preserves them quite well. Apples should feel firm and heavy for their size, but avoid those with bruises or punctured skin. Most supermarket apples are waxed, so shine isn't a good indicator of freshness, but their smell provides a good clue: fresh apples have a strong sweet scent.

Apples will keep for three weeks in the crisper or fruit drawer of your refrigerator. They occupy a spot on the Environmental Working Group's Dirty Dozen list of fruits and vegetables most contaminated with toxic pesticide residue, so purchase organic apples whenever possible, and wash them well before eating. (Note: I think organic apples also taste better than conventionally grown.)

APPLE BRUSSELS SPROUT SLAW

This dish is easy to pull together when you are in a pinch for a side dish. It's especially great during the autumn months when both Brussels sprouts and apples are in their peak season. The sweet apple nicely complements the slight bitterness of the sprouts' sulfur-containing compounds (which provide many of their health benefits).

1 tablespoon (14 g) bacon grease (from the bacon in this recipe) or coconut oil

1 pound (454 g) Brussels sprouts, trimmed and shredded or cut into ⅛-inch (3 mm) wide ribbons

1 apple, finely sliced into matchsticks

¼ teaspoon sea salt

¼ teaspoon freshly ground black pepper

2 or 3 slices nitrate-free pastured bacon, cooked and broken into pieces (optional)

In a large skillet over medium heat, add the bacon grease or coconut oil and allow to melt. Add the shredded Brussels sprouts, apple, salt, and pepper, and stir to combine. Continue to stir and cook until the Brussels sprouts are wilted down and start to turn golden, about 3 to 4 minutes. Remove from the heat and stir in the cooked bacon pieces, if using. Serve immediately.

MAKES 4 OR 5 SERVINGS

LEMONS

With their bright flavor, lemons wake up almost any dish. Arguably the world's most popular citrus fruit, lemons may have originated in northwestern India and then spread to southern Italy in 200 CE before being cultivated in Iraq and Egypt by 700 CE. But besides being an ancient food and contributing a variety of protective antioxidants to your diet, what makes lemons a Paleo superfood? Although they taste acidic, they act as a base in the body, helping you maintain the slightly alkaline blood pH (7.4, with 7.0 being neutral) at which your body functions optimally—one of the hallmarks of the fruit- and vegetable-rich Paleo diet.

IMMUNE BOOSTER

Lemons supply nearly 140 percent of the vitamin C you need every day. Because vitamin C is a water-soluble vitamin (meaning your body can't store it), lemons can help you reach your daily quota. Lemon peel contains more vitamin C than the juice or flesh, and it appears better at suppressing free radical activity, according to a laboratory study in the journal *BioFactors*. Whenever you prepare a dish with lemons, be sure to sprinkle a little grated lemon zest in as well for the most antioxidant benefit.

JUICING A LEMON

To get the most juice from a lemon, firmly roll it along a flat surface or warm it in the microwave for 15 seconds before cutting it. If you're using both zest and juice, zest the lemon first.

While vitamin C boosts your immune system, it doesn't appear to reduce your risk of getting the common cold (unless you're an elite athlete, like a marathoner, in which case getting extra vitamin C might lower your odds of getting a cold by up to 50 percent). Some studies suggest that it might shorten the duration of a cold by about 10 percent, however, should you happen to get one.

The flavonoids in lemons also help calm immunity-dampening inflammation caused by free radical attacks. Interestingly, flavonoids and vitamin C each improve the antioxidant activity of the other. Furthermore, some evidence indicates that flavonoids must be present for vitamin C to function like it's supposed to in the body.

CANCER PREVENTER

Population studies show that consuming citrus flavonoids may reduce the risk of developing certain kinds of cancer, such as stomach and pancreatic cancer. And lab studies suggest that some flavonoids in lemons, called limonoids, may protect against breast and colon cancer. Another flavonoid, naringenin, seems to stop the spread of liver cancer cells. Citrus flavonoids may help prevent cancer in three ways: by preventing the formation of new cancer cells, by keeping carcinogens from reaching sites in your body where they would be most likely to form cancerous cells, and by metabolizing carcinogens into less toxic forms or preventing their biological effects, according to a 2008 study in the *Journal of Agricultural and Food Chemistry*.

NATURAL DETOXIFIER

No matter how diligent you are with your food and personal care product choices as part of a Paleo lifestyle, in our modern world it's practically impossible to avoid exposure to environmental toxins. But there's a reason that juice cleanses and detox plans prominently feature lemons. A compound in lemons called d-limonene encourages peristalsis, or the movement of waste through your bowels, preventing toxins from lingering too long in your digestive tract. Citrus flavonoids also support your liver—your body's primary detoxifying organ—by fending off damaging free radicals and suppressing inflammation in your liver cells. And lab studies indicate that lemon extract can protect the liver by increasing levels of the antioxidant enzymes superoxide dismutase and catalase, according to a 2007 study in *Pharmaceutical Biology*.

LOOKING FOR LEMONS

You can find these sunny fruits year-round. Look for lemons with bright yellow, unwrinkled skin (a green tint may mean the lemon isn't quite ripe). The juiciest lemons have thin skin and should feel heavy for their size. Ripe lemons should also feel firm—a soft lemon is an old lemon. Choose organic lemons to reduce your exposure to toxic pesticide residue on the peel, especially if you will use the zest.

Stored in the refrigerator, lemons will last for up to three weeks. However, the volatile oils in the peel start to dissipate quickly, so don't zest a lemon until right before you'll use it. The vitamin C in lemons degrades rapidly as well, so use the remaining fruit and/or juice within two days (store it in the refrigerator in a light-blocking metal or glass container). You can also freeze the juice to preserve its vitamin C—squeeze it into an ice cube tray and freeze, then transfer the cubes to an airtight container. For this reason, it's best to squeeze your own lemon juice rather than to buy bottled juice.

MAGNIFICENT MEYERS

Originally from China, Meyer lemons are a hybrid between a lemon and a mandarin orange, which gives them a thin yellow-orange peel, a heady fragrance, and a sweeter juice that has hints of lime and mandarin—qualities that make them worth seeking out for Paleo baking.

LEMON OREGANO GRILLED CHICKEN

This simple main course is bursting with citrus flavor because you use both the zest and the juice of the vitamin C-packed lemon. Add in the flavor of garlic and oregano, and you have a delicious chicken dish that can be served a variety of ways.

5 teaspoons (18 g) lemon zest

1 tablespoon (15 ml) olive oil

1½ teaspoons dried oregano

½ teaspoon sea salt

½ teaspoon freshly ground pepper

½ teaspoon lemon juice

2 cloves garlic, minced

4 skinless, boneless chicken breasts

4 or more lemon wedges

Prepare an outdoor grill or an indoor grill pan and preheat over medium-high heat.

Combine the lemon zest, olive oil, oregano, salt, pepper, lemon juice, and garlic; rub evenly over both sides of the chicken breasts. Place the chicken on the grill and grill for 3 to 4 minutes on each side, or until the chicken is no longer pink inside. Remove from the heat.

Squeeze 1 lemon wedge evenly over each chicken breast half. Serve with additional lemon wedges, if desired.

MAKES 4 SERVINGS

TIP:

Remember to choose organic lemons to reduce your exposure to toxic pesticide residue on the peel.

CACAO

Really, you can eat chocolate on the Paleo diet? And not only can you eat it, but it's considered a Paleo superfood? Yes! (Well, a heavily qualified yes, anyway.) To be sure, our Paleolithic ancestors did not consume chocolate, and for many people that's enough of a reason not to eat it. That said, research shows that it actually has some pretty significant health benefits. So if you're looking for an indulgence, a moderate amount of chocolate (and no, a whole bar of dark chocolate is not a moderate amount!) is an excellent choice. Of course, everyone reacts differently to foods, so if you discover that chocolate gives you problems—perhaps you notice a difference in your health, or you simply can't limit yourself to a small portion—you may be better off avoiding chocolate entirely. But if you'd like to try including chocolate in your Paleo lifestyle, here's how to choose the healthiest kinds.

CACAO VERSUS COCOA

Although the terms *cacao* and *cocoa* were once used interchangeably, today cacao refers to the raw material and cocoa refers to the processed and sweetened chocolate. After harvesting pods of *Theobroma cacao* (literally, "food of the gods"), chocolate producers ferment, dry, and roast the pods, reducing their bitterness and developing their rich flavor. Then they separate the beans, or cacao nibs, from the shells and mill them into a chocolate liquid that either gets turned into cacao powder (by removing the fat, called cocoa butter) or chocolate products, with the addition of sweeteners and (often) milk solids. Many chocolate manufacturers label their products with the amount of pure cacao they contain, and the higher the percentage, the more of cacao's

health benefits you receive. If you include dark chocolate as part of your Paleo diet, I recommend choosing varieties made with at least 85 percent cacao. Raw cacao powder (not Dutch or alkalized) is an excellent option as well, especially for baking or adding to liquids such as smoothies—you may see it labeled cocoa powder, but check the ingredients to make sure there are no sweeteners or other additives. You can also find cacao nibs, which have a pleasantly bitter chocolate flavor and add a nice crunch.

FANTASTIC FLAVONOIDS

Cacao qualifies as a superfood because it contains a high concentration of antioxidant flavonoids, most notably flavonols and proanthocyanidins. In fact, per serving, cacao has a higher total antioxidant capacity than most other foods in the American diet, including other superfoods such as spinach and blueberries, according to a 2004 study in the *Journal of Agricultural and Food Chemistry*. These powerful antioxidants scavenge age-accelerating free radicals that contribute to heart disease, diabetes, obesity, cancer, and neurodegenerative conditions. For example, cacao flavonols help keep your blood vessels dilated and flexible, which protects against cardiovascular problems such as stroke and heart attack.

These antioxidants also calm inflammation (one of the main goals of the Paleo diet), which benefits nearly every system in your body. To start, cacao's anti-inflammatory effects may influence insulin resistance (reducing your risk of developing type 2 diabetes) and other conditions related to obesity, including high blood pressure and too-high levels of bad cholesterol—a trio of health problems that, together, are known as metabolic syndrome. Calming chronic inflammation also improves cardiovascular health, boosts your immune system, and protects your nerves, according to a 2011 review in the journal *Antioxidants and Redox Signaling*.

OTHER NUTRITIONAL BENEFITS

In addition to all those antioxidants, 1 ounce (28 g) of dark chocolate supplies 2 grams of protein to give your active Paleo lifestyle a little boost, 3 grams of fiber to make up for the fiber in the grains and legumes you're no longer eating, about one-quarter of the copper and manganese you need daily, and good amounts of iron and magnesium. And while cocoa butter—the fat from cacao beans—does contain saturated fat, more than half of that saturated fat is stearic acid, which doesn't raise your total cholesterol or LDL ("bad") cholesterol levels. And one-third of the total fat in cocoa butter is oleic acid, a monounsaturated fat that has a mild cholesterol-lowering effect.

CHOOSING CHOCOLATE

Look for organic cacao powder (not Dutch or alkalized) or dark chocolate bars with 85 percent cacao or higher. For dark chocolate, make sure that the bars contain only cocoa butter, a small amount of sweetener, and perhaps other natural flavorings such as vanilla—and no added emulsifiers such as soy lecithin. Good-quality dark chocolate should be smooth, rich, and intensely chocolaty, not bitter. If you find the chocolate you've chosen is too bitter for your taste, try a different brand. Take it a step further and choose Fair Trade chocolate, which ensures that farmers receive a fair price, allows them to invest in making their farms environmentally sustainable, and strictly prohibits slave and child labor (tragically common in cacao farming).

CHOCOLATE LOVER

It's not your imagination—chocolate really can make you happier. A 2009 Swiss study found that eating 40 grams (about 1.4 ounces [40 g]) of dark chocolate a day lowers the body's stress response. And cacao contains small amounts of several substances that are known to boost your mood, including calming magnesium, stimulating caffeine, serotonin-producing carbohydrates, and a mildly mood-lifting chemical called phenylethylamine (PEA) that's found in high concentrations in happy people. Of course, the stress relief might also be because chocolate is just plain delicious, which is enough to trigger an endorphin release, notes a 1999 study in *Public Health Nutrition*.

CACAO ALMOND SMOOTHIE

This creamy, delicious smoothie is packed with many of the Paleo superfoods in this book, but the cacao really shines through. This smoothie is one of my kids' favorites on a hot summer day (or night).

---

2 cups (300 g) frozen sliced bananas (about 2 to 3 bananas)

1 tablespoon (8 g) raw cacao powder

2 tablespoons (32 g) almond butter

½ teaspoon vanilla extract

1 cup (235 ml) coconut milk (see page 160) or almond milk

¼ to ½ cup (60 to 120 ml) ice-cold water

¼ teaspoon ground cinnamon

¼ cup (60 g) ice cubes

½ tablespoon honey (optional)

Combine all the ingredients in a blender and process until smooth. For the water, add ¼ cup (60 ml) first and blend. If you prefer your smoothie thick, the ¼ cup (60 ml) should be fine. If you prefer it a little thinner, then add the remaining ¼ cup (60 ml) water and blend.

Serve immediately and enjoy!

MAKES 2 SERVINGS

TIP:

Looking to add more greens to your kids' diets (or your own)? Toss in a handful of washed spinach leaves and/or one teaspoon of spirulina. It won't change the flavor—just the color!

5
PALEO SUPER FATS

People constantly ask me about the relatively high amounts of fat in the Paleo diet and admit that it's one of the reasons they're hesitant to try "going Paleo." My simple answer to most of them is, "Eating more fat won't make you fat!" After several decades of hearing the low-fat message, that might be hard to believe at first, but there's a wealth of recent research that shows that it's not only safe but extremely beneficial to include—and this is a key distinction—*good* fats in your diet. These fats (especially omega-3s and unsaturated fats) can help calm harmful inflammation, improve your cholesterol, keep your blood sugar stable, and help you feel more satisfied when you eat. They're also a critical source of calories for Paleo followers, because you're no longer consuming the grains, legumes, and dairy that make up so much of our modern diets.

Traditional hunter-gatherer societies consumed a large portion of their calories from fats—anywhere from 28 to 58 (!) percent. And research shows that a contemporary Paleo diet averages out around 39 percent of calories from fat. (For reference, most modern Western diets consist of an average of 34 percent of calories from fat, with the current recommendations for a healthy diet suggesting that people cap their intake at 30 percent.) However, "the types and balance of fats in hunter-gatherer diets would likely have been considerably different from those found in typical Western diets," notes a 2000 study in the *American Journal of Clinical Nutrition*.

What does that mean for today's Paleo followers? In the simplest terms, it means avoiding partially hydrogenated fats (trans fats) and corn, soybean, or industrial seed oils, and instead relying on the mono- and polyunsaturated fats in fruits such as avocado, coconut, and olives, and nuts and seeds—and omega-3 fats in pasture-raised animals and cold-water fatty fish as described in the "Paleo Super Proteins" chapter (see page 15). You'll notice that some of my recipes call for ghee (organic clarified butter from pasture-raised cows) or bacon grease (from organically and pasture-raised pigs), which are also fine cooking fats, but because nutritionally they don't qualify as superfoods, I've suggested superfood fats that you can use instead if you prefer.

A word on nuts and seeds: Although our ancestors gathered high-calorie, high-fat nuts and seeds to help them survive, there are a few reasons you shouldn't go overboard eating them. Besides the healthful fats, phytosterols, antioxidants, vitamins, and minerals they provide, nuts and seeds contain the anti-nutrient phytic acid (which binds to certain minerals and inhibits your body's ability to absorb them), gut-irritating lectins, and higher-than-ideal levels of pro-inflammatory omega-6 fatty acids. That said, the nuts and seeds listed in this section boast some incredible health benefits you don't want to miss out on, and most people can tolerate a handful per day of these varieties just fine.

AVOCADOS

It probably comes as no surprise that creamy, buttery avocados are high in fat—accounting for about 77 percent of their calories—but most of the fat they contain is the healthy monounsaturated kind (more on that in a minute). In addition to all those good fats, half an avocado contains a wealth of other nutrients, including 4.5 grams of fiber, 10 percent of the vitamin C you need daily, 18 percent of your vitamin K, and good amounts of the B vitamins (especially folate—with 15 percent of your recommended daily intake). It also boasts about as much potassium as a small banana, and good amounts of antioxidant vitamins and minerals such as vitamins A, C, and E, copper, and manganese.

Avocados are actually a fruit, but we tend to think of them as vegetables because that's primarily how we use them. Surprisingly versatile, mild-flavored avocados make good additions to everything from soups, salads, and egg dishes to creamy treats such as smoothies, puddings, and even Paleo brownies (the rich texture makes a great dairy substitute, and you—or your kids—will never notice the secret ingredient). Then, of course, avocados shine in spreads, salad dressings, and dips such as guacamole. With so many options, it's easy to include this Paleo superfood in your diet.

FANTASTIC FATS

Now back to those fats. Half an avocado contains about 10 grams of total fat, of which about two-thirds is monounsaturated fat and 13 percent is polyunsaturated fat—including 75 milligrams of the anti-inflammatory omega-3s so prized on the Paleo diet. Ancient hunter-gatherer societies relied on foods rich in mono- and polyunsaturated fats to sustain them, and recent research confirms that these fats can actually calm inflammation, lower your cholesterol, keep your heart rhythms steady, and lower your blood pressure. And if you needed more confirmation that the Paleo diet—free of grains and simple carbohydrates, with an emphasis on protein and healthy fats—will protect your heart, evidence shows that replacing some of the carbs in your diet with protein or unsaturated fats (especially mono-unsaturated fats such as those in avocados) reduces your risk of cardiovascular disease, according to 2005 study in the *Journal of the American Medical Association*.

Because fats take longer to digest, they give your meals and snacks "staying power," keeping you full and energized for hours. Those fats also help your body absorb fat-soluble nutrients including vitamins A, D, and E and antioxidant carotenoids. For example, study participants who ate a salad or salsa with avocado absorbed up to fifteen times as many carotenoids (including lycopene, lutein, and alpha- and beta-carotene) as participants who ate those foods without avocado, according to a 2005 study in the *Journal of Nutrition*.

FREE RADICAL–QUENCHING CAROTENOIDS

Avocados contain a number of antioxidant carotenoids, and the more fat they contain, the more carotenoids, according to a 2009 study in the *Journal of Agricultural and Food Chemistry*. The researchers also noted that the carotenoid concentration increases the closer you get to the peel, so they suggest using a "nick and peel" method to ensure you get the entire nutrient-rich outer portion: nick the skin of a whole or half avocado and peel the skin away (like you would a banana). Scientists have identified eleven different carotenoids in avocados, and these antioxidants calm inflammation; protect your body (especially your eyes, brain, and heart) from age-accelerating free-radical damage; and may reduce your risk of cancer, heart disease, and neurodegenerative diseases.

AVOCADO ABCS

There are dozens of varieties of avocados, but the most popular in the United States is the Haas variety. You'll find avocados year-round, although California-grown Haas avocados peak in the spring and summer months (95 percent of American avocados come from southern California). Because avocados mature on the tree but don't ripen until they're picked, avocados can hang out for a while and be harvested throughout the growing season. Avocados allowed to mature longer and picked later in the season contain more fat and more carotenoids.

When purchasing, avoid avocados that are overly soft or have blemished or cracked skins. You can judge an avocado's ripeness by how hard it is when you apply gentle pressure—unripe avocados will feel rock hard, and a perfectly ripe avocado should yield slightly when you press on it. Avocados ripen at room temperature within a few days. To speed the process, put your avocados in a paper bag with an apple or a banana, which emits ethylene gas that makes fruits ripen faster. If your avocados ripen before you're ready to use them, store them in the refrigerator for two or three days.

IT AIN'T EASY STAYING GREEN

Exposure to oxygen turns avocado flesh an unappetizing brown. The best way to prevent this oxidation is with an acidic agent such as lemon or lime juice—either blending it into puréed avocado or coating the surface of cut pieces. If you only need, say, half an avocado for a recipe, sprinkle or brush juice over the cut half and wrap it tightly with plastic wrap before storing in the refrigerator (use it within a day). And although fresh avocados have a better texture, you can freeze avocado purée (use a ratio of 1 tablespoon [15 ml] lemon or lime juice for each avocado) for up to five months for later use in dips, spreads, and smoothies. If you still notice a little browning, simply scrape off the oxidized part and enjoy the rest.

AVOCADO TOMATO TARTS

Avocado is a nutrient booster—its healthy fats enable your body to absorb more of the fat-soluble nutrients in the foods you eat with it. For example, eating avocado with tomatoes, as in this recipe, helps your body absorb up to fifteen times more lycopene from the tomatoes.

FOR AVOCADO TOMATO SALAD:

1 pint (300 g) cherry tomatoes, halved

2 scallions, finely diced

1 clove garlic, minced

Juice of 1 lemon

2 tablespoons (30 ml) olive oil

Sea salt and freshly ground pepper to taste

1 or 2 avocados, diced

¼ cup (10 g) fresh basil, chopped

2 tablespoons (8 g) fresh oregano, chopped

FOR TARTS:

⅓ cup (80 g) coconut oil, melted

1 clove garlic, minced

½ tablespoon fresh basil, finely chopped

½ tablespoon fresh oregano, finely chopped

2 pasture-raised eggs

¼ teaspoon sea salt

½ cup (60 g) coconut flour

To make the salad: In a large bowl, combine the tomatoes, scallions, garlic, lemon juice, olive oil, salt, and pepper. Toss to combine. Gently stir in the avocado, basil, and oregano. Place in an airtight container in the refrigerator until you're ready to assemble the tarts.

To make the tarts: Preheat the oven to 350°F (180°C, or gas mark4). Grease 6 individual tart pans with butter from grass-fed cows or coconut oil. You can also use a large tart pan if desired. If using small tart pans, place them on a baking sheet.

Combine all the tart ingredients in a bowl and mix with a fork to incorporate. The mixture should come together into a dough-like texture.

Press the dough into the greased tart pans, covering the bottom and up the sides. Bake for 10 to 12 minutes, or until slightly golden. Allow the tarts to cool in their pans. Remove them carefully from the pans and let them come to room temperature.

Fill the tarts with the avocado tomato salad and sprinkle with additional herbs, if desired. Another delicious topping is cooked and diced bacon.

MAKES 6 TARTS

COCONUT

Coconut products, such as oil, milk, butter, flour, and dried coconut meat, are incredibly versatile, and many Paleo enthusiasts consume them as their main source of dietary fat. Coconut oil's high concentration of saturated fat means it's quite stable at high temperatures and is less prone to oxidative damage, making it great for cooking. Coconut milk makes a wonderful dairy substitute, and you can swap in coconut flour for some grain flours in baking.

In addition to providing fat, coconut meat supplies good amounts of several minerals, especially the antioxidant manganese. Keep in mind that coconut does contain some phytic acid (although much less than most other tree nuts), which inhibits absorption of certain minerals—most notably iron, zinc, and magnesium—and can cause problems for some people with autoimmune conditions. Overall, though, coconut is a first-rate fat that most Paleo followers enjoy with no problems.

MEDIUM-CHAIN FATTY ACIDS

Nutrition experts have long advised avoiding coconut because of its high saturated fat content (more than 90 percent of its total fat) and fears that it would raise cholesterol levels and increase heart disease risk. However, although coconut oil does contain saturated fatty acids that increase cholesterol, a good portion of coconut's saturated fats are in the form of lauric acid and other medium-chain fatty acids that may actually boost your HDL ("good") cholesterol. Coconut oil also appears to lower levels of lipoprotein(a), a type of cholesterol linked to cardiovascular risk, according to a 2003 study in the *Journal of Nutrition*. If you're following a Paleo lifestyle, which minimizes chronic low-grade inflammation, the mild increase in total

cholesterol levels from coconut shouldn't pose a problem, concludes Loren Cordain, Ph.D., professor of health and exercise science at Colorado State University and author of *The Paleo Diet*.

Those medium-chain fatty acids have other benefits as well. Because they don't require bile acids for digestion, your body can metabolize them easily for a ready source of energy that won't cause a spike in your blood sugar. The lauric acid in coconut oil also has antibacterial, antiviral, antifungal, and antioxidant properties. In addition, lauric acid appears to inhibit cyclooxygenase-1 (COX-1) and cyclooxygenase-2 (COX-2), enzymes associated with inflammation and pain.

CRAZY FOR COCONUT

Coconut comes in a variety of forms you can use in your Paleo kitchen. I keep these five coconut products in my home at all times.

EXTRA-VIRGIN COCONUT OIL: This mildly sweet, fragrant oil provides a beautiful flavor to baked dishes. Unlike most other plant oils, coconut oil has a high melting point (about 76° to 78°F, or 24° to 25°C), so coconut oil stays solid until temperatures go above that range—which means that if you purchase a bottle of liquid coconut oil and it turns solid, don't think that it's gone bad. And of course, don't store it in your refrigerator!

COCONUT FLOUR: This Paleo kitchen staple is very useful for Paleo baking and for thickening sauces. Coconut flour is made by grinding coconut pulp after it has been squeezed for coconut milk, which produces a soft flour. It's high in fiber, protein, and fat, which makes it exceptionally filling.

COCONUT MILK: Coconut milk is the liquid pressed out of coconut meat. It makes a great dairy alternative, especially for baking. In my recipes, I use canned, full-fat, unsweetened coconut milk. As it sits, the fat and water separate, so before using be sure to shake it to bring it back together. If it is the coconut cream you're after, don't shake the can before opening, and scrape off the cream that accumulates at the top of the can (you can reserve the water for another use). Look for cans that are labeled free of bisphenol-A (BPA), an endocrine disrupter; purchase coconut milk sold in cartons (see Resources, page 214); or make your own (see recipe, page 160).

COCONUT BUTTER: This is a purée of whole coconut flesh (not just the oil) that's a little fibrous and has a texture similar to slightly grainy almond butter (see bonus recipe to make your own). During storage, the coconut oil may separate and form a solid top layer on the coconut butter—if this happens, simply warm it a little and blend it back together.

UNSWEETENED COCONUT FLAKES AND UNSWEET-ENED SHREDDED COCONUT: Unsweetened coconut is fairly brittle and has a longer shelf life than sweetened varieties. Shredded coconut is a very small cut, suitable for baking, while coconut flakes are larger pieces, perfect for garnishes or toppings.

BONUS RECIPE

COCONUT BUTTER

Coconut butter is a little scoop of heaven, but if you buy it from the store it can be pricey. This recipe is so easy and inexpensive that I don't feel guilty about making (and eating!) it whenever I want.

1 package (8 ounces, or 224 g) organic unsweetened dried coconut flakes

1½ tablespoons (21 g) coconut oil, melted

In a food processor or blender, place the coconut flakes and coconut oil. Process for about 10 minutes, or until the coconut butter gets creamy, stopping halfway through to scrape down the sides of the processor or blender. Your food processor will be nice and hot after making your coconut butter, but it's worth it!

MAKES ABOUT 1 CUP (224 G)

Note: I like to add ½ teaspoon ground cinnamon (or more) to this recipe, and some of my blog readers have included other flavorings, such as nutmeg or vanilla extract. Feel free to experiment!

MAKE YOUR OWN

Most commercial brands of coconut milk contain guar gum—made from guar beans—as a thickener and stabilizer. Many people tolerate guar gum just fine, but if you find it causes digestive problems, you should seek out a brand of coconut milk without this additive (see Resources, page 214) or make your own, which also solves the problem of BPA exposure from canned coconut milk (see recipe, page 160). It's relatively simple to make your own coconut milk and coconut butter using coconut flakes and a high-powered blender or food processor. It's also much less expensive.

HOMEMADE COCONUT MILK

This naturally sweetened coconut milk is easy to make and it doesn't have any of the additives in canned versions. And unlike traditional dairy products, which trigger inflammation, coconut milk contains lauric acid—a medium-chain saturated fat—that actually inhibits certain inflammatory enzymes. Add it to smoothies or coffee, or enjoy on its own.

2 cups (170 g) organic unsweetened dried coconut flakes

2 Medjool dates, pitted

4 cups (940 ml) hot filtered water (not boiling)

1 teaspoon vanilla extract (optional)

Place the coconut flakes and dates in a deep, heatproof glass bowl and pour the hot water over to cover. Let steep for 1 to 2 hours, on the counter.

Place the coconut mixture and vanilla extract, if using, in a blender. Blend for 2 minutes until everything is smooth.

Line a metal strainer with cheesecloth and place it over a glass bowl. Pour the coconut mixture into the lined strainer, then squeeze the coconut pulp to get every last drop of coconut milk out. Pour the coconut milk into glass mason jars for storing. Coconut milk can be kept in the refrigerator for up to 1 week. The milk will separate in the refrigerator, so shake before serving.

MAKES ⅔ TO ¾ CUP (160 TO 180 ML)

TIDBIT:

Delicious on its own, you can also add this coconut milk to smoothies or coffee, or use it to make hot chocolate. For hot chocolate, warm 1⅝ cups (385 ml) of coconut milk in a saucepan over medium-low heat until milk is thoroughly heated. Add 2½ tablespoons (11 g) cacao powder, 3–4 teaspoons (21–28 g) honey (or maple syrup), ¼ teaspoon cinnamon, and a pinch of sea salt. Whisk until smooth and then remove from heat. Divide into two mugs and serve with a sprinkle of cacao and a cinnamon stick for garnish.

ALMONDS

Technically a seed (of the fruit of the almond tree), almonds have gained quite a reputation as a superfood, and for good reason. One ounce (28 g) of almonds (about 23, or a handful) provides 3.4 grams of cholesterol-clearing fiber, 6 grams of muscle-building protein, and good amounts of energizing iron and bone-strengthening calcium (especially important in the dairy-free Paleo diet!). They also supply more than a third of your daily vitamin E quota and nearly all of the B vitamins, and they're a super source of the antioxidant mineral manganese, plus copper, magnesium, and phosphorus. Almonds also boast significant amounts of phytonutrients, especially plant sterols and flavonoids, which provide additional health benefits.

Paleolithic hunter-gatherers consumed nuts and seeds—including almonds—as a regular part of their diets, and almonds continue to be a popular Paleo snack today (ground almonds, also called almond meal, make a great substitute for grain flours). Almonds are a superfood, after all, and it's hard to beat their convenience. But don't go overboard. For one thing, almonds are a concentrated source of calories. Even more importantly, they contain far more inflammation-promoting omega-6 fatty acids than the beneficial omega-3s that the Paleo diet emphasizes. In the context of a diet rich in wild-caught fish and grass-fed meat, which provide high amounts of omega-3s, most people can safely enjoy small quantities of almonds and all of the nutrients they provide. However, if inflammation is a significant problem for you (for instance, if you have an autoimmune condition), you may want to limit your intake. That said, here are some of the ways almonds benefit your health.

PROTECT YOUR HEART

Numerous studies show that eating almonds can lower your total cholesterol levels and your levels of LDL ("bad") cholesterol. Almonds may reduce your heart disease risk in other ways as well. In an Iranian study of thirty men with mildly high cholesterol, eating 2 ounces (56 g) of almonds a day (which is admittedly more than you'll want to eat) for four weeks significantly lowered their total and LDL cholesterol, as well as other lipid risk factors for coronary heart disease, including the likelihood that those lipids would undergo oxidative damage.

Almonds can also help regulate your blood pressure. One ounce (28 g) of almonds contains just a trace of sodium, which is one of the main culprits behind hypertension, and nearly 200 milligrams of potassium, which counteracts the blood pressure–raising effects of sodium. And you might notice this benefit quickly—volunteers who ate a diet high in almonds lowered their systolic and diastolic blood pressure in just two weeks, according to a 2008 study in the *European Journal of Nutrition*. Almonds' high potassium content means they fit right in with the contemporary Paleo diet, which boasts about 12.5 times more potassium than sodium.

BOOST YOUR ENERGY

One ounce (28 g) of almonds offers 6 grams of high-quality carbohydrates to provide energy without triggering an insulin spike that raises your risk of cardiovascular disease and blood sugar problems such as type 2 diabetes—a main benefit of the Paleo diet. Almonds also provide B vitamins, copper, iron, and high amounts of manganese, which all contribute to your body's ability to metabolize fats and carbohydrates for energy. In addition, manganese and copper are components of the antioxidant enzyme superoxide dismutase (SOD), which is especially effective at fighting free radicals in your cells' mitochondria (your main energy producers) so they can do their job.

BUYING AND STORING ALMONDS

Because of almonds' high fat content, you'll need to take care when purchasing and storing to keep them from going rancid. Fresh almonds should smell sweet and nutty—a sharp or bitter odor may mean they're past their prime. Organic almonds contain less of the anti-nutrient phytic acid because they're grown without modern high-phosphate fertilizers (phytic acid is the storage form of phosphorus for many plants, including almonds). You can also purchase blanched almonds to minimize the phytic acid content, because the brown skins contain most of almonds' phytic acid. Once you get almonds home, store them in an airtight container in a cool, dry place away from sunlight. To extend their shelf life, you can also keep them in the refrigerator (for a few months) or the freezer (for up to a year).

HAVE YOU GONE NUTS FOR NUTS?

One trick to keep your nut and seed consumption in check is to buy them still in the shell, because the act of shelling will slow you down and keep you from consuming too many at a time.

If you like roasted nuts, choose dry-roasted varieties to avoid extra oil. And read the ingredients label to make sure there are no additives such as sugar, corn syrup, or preservatives. You can also buy raw almonds and toast them yourself in a 325°F (170°C, or gas mark 3) oven for 20 to 25 minutes, or until golden brown and fragrant. This gives you the flexibility of adding any herbs or spices you want, which is an excellent way to sneak in additional Paleo superfoods—get creative!

ROASTED ROSEMARY SPICED ALMONDS

Roasting nuts brings out their natural oils and really brightens up their flavor. These almonds are smoky, lightly salted, and fragrant with rosemary, making them the perfect Paleo snack for your gatherings.

½ tablespoon olive oil

1 tablespoon (1.7 g) fresh rosemary, finely chopped, plus extra for garnish

¼ teaspoon sea salt

⅛ teaspoon cayenne pepper

⅛ teaspoon paprika

1 cup (145 g) raw organic almonds

Preheat the oven to 325°F (170°C, or gas mark 3). Line a baking sheet with parchment paper and set aside.

In a small bowl, combine the olive oil, rosemary, sea salt, cayenne pepper, and paprika. Add the almonds and toss to combine and evenly coat.

Spread the almonds in an even layer on the prepared baking sheet. Roast for 25 to 30 minutes, until the almonds are lightly toasted and fragrant. Allow the almonds to cool for 5 to 10 minutes. The almonds will harden once cooled.

Sprinkle the almonds with additional rosemary (if desired) and serve. The almonds will keep in an airtight container or jar for 7 to 10 days.

MAKES 1 CUP (145 G)

TIP:

This recipe can be doubled or tripled and packaged as a great gift for the holidays. Simply scoop the almonds into glass mason jars and add decorative labels and ribbon.

WALNUTS

Walnuts might just be the oldest tree food known to man, and our ancestors gathered them for survival. Their cultivation dates back to the ancient Romans and Persians, and walnuts were a valuable commodity along the Silk Road trade route between Asia and the Middle East. Although widely available today, these delicious nuts still deserve their prized status for all of the nutrients (and, as a result, health benefits) they provide. In addition to their protein, fiber, vitamins, and minerals, walnuts supply a good amount of beneficial omega-3 fatty acids, making them a true Paleo superfood.

THE SKINNY ON FAT

One ounce (about 14 halves, or 28 g) of walnuts provides 2,565 milligrams of omega-3 fatty acids in the form of alpha-linolenic acid (ALA). ALA is a kind of omega-3 fat found in plant foods, and your body can convert it into eicosapentaenoic acid (EPA) and docosahexaenoic acid (DHA), the omega-3 fats found in cold-water fatty fish such as salmon. These remarkable fats can calm inflammation, which helps ease conditions like arthritis and asthma, and reduces your risk of heart disease and stroke. In fact, omega-3s protect your cardiovascular system in several ways—by lowering cholesterol and blood pressure, and by lessening your chances of having a fatal heart attack. Omega-3s have also been shown to boost brain function, potentially improving conditions such as depression, attention deficit hyperactivity disorder (ADHD), and Alzheimer's disease. As if that weren't enough, omega-3s can also help you achieve the Paleo goal of improved blood sugar control. Consuming 1 ounce (28 g) of walnuts at least twice a week could reduce your

risk of developing type 2 diabetes by up to 15 percent, according to a very large population study published in 2013 in the *Journal of Nutrition*.

That doesn't give you license to eat walnuts with abandon, however. Like all nuts and seeds, walnuts do contain anti-nutrients such as phytic acid that can inhibit mineral absorption and cause digestive distress. And walnuts contain inflammation-promoting omega-6 fatty acids in addition to their omega-3s, in a ratio of about 4:1. Although that's higher than the Paleo ideal of 2:1 or 1:1, it's the best out of all the nuts and seeds, making walnuts an excellent choice.

NATURE'S STRESS BUSTER

Stress seems unavoidable these days, but eating walnuts can help make you more resilient against its harmful effects. Consuming enough of the omega-3 fatty acid DHA may help reduce the impact of stress on brain function, partly by improving the brain's ability to repair itself, according to a 2013 study in *Ageing Research Reviews*. Another recent study found that eating walnuts and walnut oil can help buffer the effects of stress on your blood pressure. Researchers measured the cardiovascular responses of study participants who gave a speech or immersed their feet in cold water. Those who ate walnuts had lower blood pressure and improved cardiovascular markers compared with those who ate an average American diet.

A HANDFUL OF ANTIOXIDANTS

Walnuts consistently rank as one of the most antioxidant-rich plant foods in studies. In 2013, researchers at the University of Scranton compared nine different types of nuts and found that walnuts had the highest levels of total polyphenols (plant-based antioxidants). Those antioxidants inhibit the oxidation of LDL ("bad") cholesterol and reduce your risk of atherosclerosis. They also provide brain benefits: walnut extract and alpha-linolenic acid protect against age-related cellular dysfunction and cell death in hippocampus cells, according to a 2013 study in the journal *Nutritional Neuroscience*.

KEEP 'EM COLD!

Because of their high fat content, walnuts go rancid quickly. Make sure that wherever you purchase your walnuts has high product turnover so you get the freshest nuts, and smell them if possible. Rancid nuts have an unappetizing odor reminiscent of paint thinner. Whether you purchase them in the shell, packaged, or in bulk, the best way to preserve walnuts' freshness is to keep them cold—either in the refrigerator (for a few months) or the freezer (for up to a year). Walnuts absorb the flavors of other foods, so store them in an airtight container away from foods with strong odors. Purchasing walnuts in the shell will also extend their shelf life (in-shell walnuts are easiest to find during the fall and early winter, just after harvesting). Along the same lines, wait to chop or grind walnuts until you need to use them.

HOW TO TOAST WALNUTS

Whether you use your oven or your stove top, toasting walnuts enhances their flavor (and will make your whole house smell delicious). To toast walnuts in your oven, preheat it to 350°F (180°C, or gas mark 4) and spread out the walnuts in a single layer on a baking sheet. Bake for 8 to 10 minutes, or until fragrant and lightly browned. On the stove top, pour the walnuts into a dry skillet and toast over medium-high heat for 3 to 5 minutes, stirring frequently and watching closely so they don't burn.

MEXICAN CHOCOLATE WALNUT SNACK BARS

These are known as a snack-on-the-go in my house, especially for my kids during those busy summer months—they love them, and I love that I know what is in them! I've found it helps to freeze these before heading out so they are perfect by the time you are ready to eat them.

1¼ cups (222 g) pitted and chopped Medjool dates

¾ cup (109 g) toasted almonds

½ cup (75 g) toasted walnuts

¼ cup (35 g) toasted pumpkin seeds

3 tablespoons (24 g) cacao powder

1 teaspoon ground cinnamon

Pinch of salt

Place all the ingredients into a food processor and process until a paste forms. If a paste doesn't form, add 1 tablespoon (15 ml) of water and continue to process until a paste or dough forms.

Line a loaf pan with parchment paper, and press the date mixture into the pan. Place in the refrigerator for about 15 to 20 minutes to help the bars form. They will also be easier to cut into bars when they are a little cold.

Remove the parchment paper from the pan, and slice the date mixture into bars. (I cut some of them in half for a perfect kid-size snack.)

Wrap up the bars individually in the parchment and tie them with string. Then place the bars in an airtight container and store them in the refrigerator or freezer. If you keep them in the freezer, you can enjoy them frozen or allow the bars to come to room temperature before eating.

MAKES 8 BARS

TIP:

To toast nuts and seeds, preheat the oven to 350°F (180°C, or gas mark 4). Evenly distribute them on a baking sheet and bake for about 5 minutes, or until fragrant and lightly golden. Be careful not to overcook and burn them.

PUMPKIN SEEDS

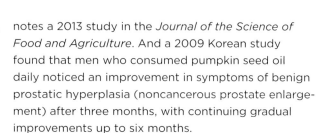

Native to North America, pumpkin seeds are a quint-essential fall treat now popular the world over. Known in Latin America as pepitas, these flat green seeds have a chewy texture and a slightly nutty flavor that makes them a great addition to recipes or delicious as a snack by themselves. Some varieties of pumpkins produce their seeds encased in a yellow-white shell or husk, which is edible as well, although most people prefer to eat just the kernel inside. (To do that, you just pop the whole thing in your mouth and crack open the shell with your teeth to get at the seed.)

These ancient seeds are great fuel for an active Paleo lifestyle—not only are they high in muscle-building protein (with 9 grams per ounce [28 g]), but they also contain high levels of iron and magnesium, minerals that boost muscle function and give you loads of energy. Pumpkin seeds provide plenty of other minerals as well, including antioxidant manganese (42 percent of your recommended daily intake), phosphorus (33 percent), copper (19 percent), and zinc (14 percent). Those are impressive amounts, even considering that the anti-nutrient phytic acid and lignans that pumpkin seeds also contain will block some of the absorption of several of these minerals.

PROTECT YOUR PROSTATE

Cultures around the world use pumpkin seeds (and pumpkin seed oil) to support prostate health. Pumpkin seeds contain a form of vitamin E called gamma-tocopherol that may protect against colon and prostate cancer. Pumpkin seeds also contain antioxidant carotenoids such as lutein and zeaxanthin, which, along with the alpha- and gamma-tocopherols, may protect against other prostate diseases as well,

notes a 2013 study in the *Journal of the Science of Food and Agriculture*. And a 2009 Korean study found that men who consumed pumpkin seed oil daily noticed an improvement in symptoms of benign prostatic hyperplasia (noncancerous prostate enlargement) after three months, with continuing gradual improvements up to six months.

KEEP CALM

Pumpkin seeds contain high amounts of the amino acid tryptophan, which your body uses to make serotonin, a neurotransmitter that boosts mood and helps you relax. Pumpkin seeds are an especially effective source because they're also rich in the zinc your brain needs to convert tryptophan into serotonin. (Eating pumpkin seeds with a little bit of healthy carbohydrate will help even more of the tryptophan reach your brain.)

The magnesium in pumpkin seeds also helps you stay calm and relaxed. Most people in the United States don't get enough magnesium in their diets, which can contribute to a shortage of serotonin that leads to irritability, anxiety, and trouble sleeping. But research shows that magnesium might relieve depression as well as tricyclic antidepressants do.

HELP YOUR HEART

The nutrients in pumpkin seeds benefit your cardio-vascular health in several ways. To start, pumpkin seeds' monounsaturated and polyunsaturated fats can help lower your cholesterol. (And some of those polyunsaturated fats are heart-protective omega-3s, although the ratio of inflammatory omega-6s to omega-3s is closer to 10:1 than the Paleo ideal of 2:1 or 1:1.) They also contain good amounts of phytos-terols, plant compounds that are structurally similar to your body's cholesterol. They're similar enough, in fact, that they compete with cholesterol for absorp-tion in your digestive system, thereby lowering your blood cholesterol levels.

The magnesium in pumpkin seeds helps lower your blood pressure and keeps your heart rhythm steady, reducing your risk of sudden cardiac death. And pumpkin seed oil lowers blood pressure and protects the cardiovascular system, according to a 2012 animal study in the *Journal of Medicinal Food*.

PICKING PERFECT PUMPKIN SEEDS

You can find pumpkin seeds packaged or in bulk bins at the market, or you can reserve them from pumpkins you use for other purposes. If you're buying your pumpkin seeds, make sure there's no trace of moisture or insect damage (and smell them if you can, to make sure they're not rancid or musty), and choose organic raw seeds whenever possible. Likewise, opt for organic whole pumpkins if you're saving the seeds. Purchasing raw seeds will allow you to control the roasting time and temperature (so all those good fats stay intact), and you can season them to your liking. Store pumpkin seeds—both raw and roasted—in an airtight container in the refrigerator to keep their oils from going rancid. They should keep for about six months (or up to a year in the freezer), but I think they're best within the first month or two.

ROAST YOUR OWN PUMPKIN SEEDS

Whether you're carving a jack-o'-lantern or prepar-ing a delicious autumn recipe, don't throw away your pumpkin seeds—it's easy to roast your own! Simply scoop them out, rinse them well, and lay them out in a single layer to dry completely (preferably over-night). When you're ready to roast, preheat your oven to 250°F (120°C, or gas mark ½). Spread the seeds in a single layer on a rimmed baking sheet and roast, stirring occasionally, for 50 minutes (this temperature and timing best preserves the seeds' fats and antioxidants, according to a 2012 study in the *Journal of Food Science*). While roasted pump-kin seeds are delicious plain, for variety you can also experiment by taking the seeds out of the oven after 25 minutes and tossing them with 1 tablespoon (14 g) of coconut or olive oil and your desired spice blend before popping them back in the oven to finish cooking.

PUMPKIN SEED TRAIL MIX

For a simple on-the-go bite, enjoy a handful of this trail mix—the nuts, seeds, and fruit will boost your energy and keep you from feeling ravenous.

1 cup (140 g) raw pumpkin seeds

½ cup (75 g) almonds, chopped

⅓ cup (50 g) walnuts

⅓ cup (50 g) pecans

1 tablespoon (14 g) coconut oil, melted

1 tablespoon (15 ml) maple syrup

1 teaspoon ground cinnamon

¼ teaspoon sea salt

¼ cup (about 4, or 45 g) pitted and chopped Medjool dates

½ cup (40 g) unsweetened large coconut flakes, lightly toasted

Preheat the oven to 325°F (170°C, or gas mark 3). Line 2 baking sheets with parchment paper and set aside.

In a large bowl, toss the pumpkin seeds, almonds, walnuts, and pecans with the coconut oil, maple syrup, cinnamon, and sea salt until evenly coated.

Spread the nuts and seeds in an even single layer on the lined baking sheets. Bake, stirring several times with a spatula or wooden spoon, until just golden, about 30 to 35 minutes.

Cool the nuts completely on the pan, then add the dates and toasted coconut flakes and toss to combine. Store cooled trail mix in an airtight container at room temperature.

MAKES 3 CUPS (435 G)

TIP:

To toast coconut flakes, preheat the oven to 325°F (170°C, or gas mark 3). Spread the coconut flakes out in a single layer on a baking sheet lined with parchment paper and bake for 5 to 10 minutes until lightly golden. Be sure to check the flakes often so they do not burn.

SUNFLOWER SEEDS

Sunflowers may have been domesticated as early as 2600 BCE in Mexico, and as they spread, they became especially prized in eastern North America as a primary source of dietary fat. Although we no longer need nuts and seeds to fuel an intense day of hunting or foraging for our next meal, sunflower seeds supply slow-burning energy, muscle-building protein, antioxidant vitamins and minerals, and phytosterols (plant compounds that lower cholesterol)—all of which help ward off modern diseases such as heart disease, cancer, and obesity. Our ancestors valued the seeds of this beautiful flower for several reasons, which, taken together, earn them the title of Paleo superfood today.

Of course, for all their benefits, sunflower seeds do contain inflammation-triggering omega-6 fatty acids. As with all nuts and seeds, moderation is the name of the game. Along those lines, I recommend purchasing sunflower seeds in the shell, because shelling them is time-consuming and will keep you from eating too many at once.

KEEP CALM AND WORK HARD

Imagine being able to stay alert and focused throughout a long day of work, without stressing out or craving sugar, caffeine, or other Paleo no-nos for a quick fix. Or maybe you'd like to power through a tough workout and not feel totally depleted afterward. Sound good? Then sunflower seeds are your go-to snack. Sunflower seeds provide a great mix of dietary fiber, protein, and complex carbohydrates to give you a steady supply of energy and help you build muscle. Sunflower seeds also supply magnesium (about a quarter of your daily quota in 1 ounce [28 g] of seeds), which helps your body produce energy and keeps your muscles working properly.

The tiny kernels are a good sources of several B vitamins, including thiamin, niacin, B_6, and folate, which help your body convert blood sugar into energy. And they contain a good amount of tryptophan, an amino acid that your body uses to produce serotonin. Serotonin is sometimes called a "feel-good" neurotransmitter because it helps regulate your mood and your sleep/wake cycles. A little serotonin boost can help you stay relaxed but focused—kind of an ideal state!

SOAKING NUTS AND SEEDS

Nuts and seeds can be difficult for some people to digest because they're high in digestive-enzyme inhibitors (such as lectins and phytic acid), although they contain far less of these compounds than grains and soy do. Traditional cultures often soaked and then dehydrated their nuts and seeds to make them easier to digest—a technique that you can easily reproduce at home. Simply cover your nuts or seeds in clean water and soak overnight or for up to eighteen hours, then rinse them off and dry them out in a food dehydrator or a very low-temperature oven. Roasting them at this point may reduce the phytic acid content even further.

AMP UP THE ANTIOXIDANTS

One ounce (28 g) of sunflower seeds provides about a quarter of your daily allowance of the antioxidant minerals copper, manganese, and selenium. But vitamin E is the real antioxidant superstar in sunflower seeds. Many people in the United States don't consume enough vitamin E in their diets. That may increase the risk of developing heart disease, cancer, and eye problems such as age-related macular degeneration, according to population studies. Severe shortages may even lead to nerve damage, muscle weakness, and loss of muscle mass. And supplements don't seem to show much benefit, possibly because most only provide one form of vitamin E, called alpha-tocopherol, and not the other seven forms. But sunflower seeds are a very good source of vitamin E—just 1 ounce (28 g) of seed kernels provides nearly half of the amount you need daily. This fat-soluble vitamin helps quench cell-damaging free radicals throughout your body, boosts your immune system so it can defend against bacteria and viruses, widens your blood vessels and prevents dangerous clotting, and helps your cells communicate with each other.

SHOPPING FOR SUNFLOWER SEEDS

You can find sunflower seeds still in the shell or sold as kernels, prepackaged or in bulk, and raw or toasted. If you purchase unshelled sunflower seeds, check to make sure that the shells aren't broken or dirty. With shelled seeds, watch for yellowing—it's a sign that the kernels might be going rancid. If you buy your seeds in bulk, give them the sniff test to check for rancidity (and make sure that the bulk bins are covered and that the store has good product turnover so you're getting fresh seeds). Like other nuts and seeds that have a high fat content, sunflower seeds keep best at cold temperatures. Store them in an airtight container in the refrigerator or freezer for the longest shelf life.

A NOTE ON SEED OILS

Most people tolerate small amounts of nuts and seeds just fine, even though they contain the potentially problematic components phytic acid, lectins, and omega-6 fatty acids. However, those substances (especially the inflammatory omega-6 fats) get concentrated when you extract the oil. Because the oil is mostly made up of fragile polyunsaturated fats, it's also very susceptible to heat damage. During industrial seed oil processing, the oils are generally heated to very high temperatures (and extracted with chemical solvents, chemically deodorized, refined, and so on). That means by the time they reach the supermarket, they may be already in the process of becoming rancid, or oxidized. Oxidized polyunsaturated fatty acids are actually one of the biggest contributors to inflammatory diseases, including heart disease, which is why the Paleo diet generally does not include seed oils.

SUNFLOWER SEED BUTTER

Sunflower seed butter is versatile and filled with nutrients. It's also a good option for anyone allergic to nuts. In fact, sunflower seed butter has significantly more unsaturated fat, magnesium, zinc, iron, and vitamin E than peanut butter does.

Preheat the oven to 350°F (180°C, or gas mark 4).

Spread the sunflower seeds on a large baking sheet in a thin layer. Bake for 10 to 15 minutes. After the first 5 minutes, rotate the baking sheet every 3 minutes until the seeds are golden brown. Remove from the oven and let cool for a couple of minutes.

Add the roasted seeds to the bowl of your food processor or high-powered blender. Begin to process or blend. While the machine is running, add the oil (1 tablespoon [14 g] at first) and salt. If you feel that your butter needs a bit more liquefying, add up to the remaining 1 tablespoon (14 g). Continue processing or blending for a total of 10 to 12 minutes, pausing every few minutes to scrape down the sides of the bowl.

Store the sunflower seed butter in an airtight container in the fridge for up to 2 weeks.

MAKES 3 CUPS (435 G)

3 cups (435 g) raw, unsalted hulled sunflower seeds

1 to 2 tablespoons (14 to 28 g) coconut oil, melted

¼ teaspoon sea salt

CHANGE IT UP

Add ½ teaspoon of a spice such as cinnamon, pumpkin pie spice, or other favorite spices to add a different flavor to the butter. Want it sweeter? You can also add 1 tablespoon of honey or maple syrup.

MACADAMIA NUTS

As you might guess from their luxuriously creamy texture, macadamia nuts are high in fat—higher than most nuts and seeds, in fact. This was great news for the aboriginal Australians, who needed fat- and calorie-dense foods to sustain them. And it's great news for us, too: Most of the fat in macadamia nuts is monounsaturated, which lowers your total cholesterol and your LDL ("bad") cholesterol while raising your HDL ("good") cholesterol. In fact, men and women with mildly elevated cholesterol levels who ate a diet rich in macadamia nuts for five weeks reduced their total cholesterol and LDL levels, thereby lowering their risk of cardiovascular disease, according to a 2008 study in the *Journal of Nutrition*. But more on macadamia nuts' healthy fats in a minute.

Macadamia nuts are also a good source of several vitamins and minerals, plus fiber and protein that promotes satiety, or the feeling of fullness and satisfaction. A bonus: The monounsaturated fats in macadamia nuts boost your body's absorption of other nutrients—especially fat-soluble vitamins (A, D, and E) and the antioxidant carotenoids. So snack on a handful, sprinkle chopped macadamia nuts over salads or vegetable side dishes, or use them to make a crunchy coating for chicken or fish. And macadamia nut oil (see sidebar) is a flavorful, versatile option for cooking and finishing dishes as well.

FOCUS ON FATS

Macadamia nuts contain a decent amount (58 milligrams per ounce [28 g]) of omega-3 fatty acids, those Paleo-prized polyunsaturated fats that calm inflammation, protect your heart, keep your brain healthy, and improve blood sugar control. And although they do contain some inflammation-promoting omega-6s, the ratio of omega-6s to omega-3s is 6:1, which is better than most tree nuts (but admittedly still a ways off from the Paleo ideal of 2:1 or even 1:1, so you still need to keep your portions in check).

Macadamia nuts also provide some other noteworthy fats. For example, they're an unusually rich source of the monounsaturated fat palmitoleic acid, which is also called omega-7 fatty acid. Animal studies suggest that palmitoleic acid can improve insulin sensitivity so your body can better regulate your blood sugar levels, and can lower triglyceride levels (high triglycerides are one of the symptoms of diabetes and other blood sugar disorders that contribute to the risk of heart disease).

And then there's oleic acid, a monounsaturated fatty acid also found in olive oil that's partly responsible for olive oil's reputation as a heart-healthy choice because it helps lower cholesterol levels. Research suggests it may also protect you against certain types of cancer, such as colon and breast cancer, and help calm inflammation, showing particular benefit for the immune system and inflammatory diseases.

OTHER NUTRITIONAL HIGHLIGHTS

One ounce (28 g) of macadamia nuts supplies nearly a quarter of your recommended daily allowance of thiamin, or vitamin B_1. Thiamin helps your body metabolize the carbohydrates, fats, and proteins in your food, and you need it to form adenosine triphosphate (ATP), which your cells use for energy. Like the other B vitamins, thiamin supports your immune system and helps your body respond better to stressful situations, qualities that earn the Bs the nickname "the anti-stress vitamins."

Macadamia nuts also provide more than half of the manganese that you should get daily, and about 10 percent of your daily quota of copper. These minerals are antioxidants in their own right, but they're also precursors of the enzyme superoxide dismutase (SOD) produced in your mitochondria. SOD is a powerful free radical fighter, combating the oxidative stress that may lead to chronic disease, including osteoporosis, type 2 diabetes, neurodegenerative diseases, cardiovascular disease, and cancer.

The magnesium in macadamia nuts plays a critical role in nerve and muscle function, including keeping your heart rhythm steady. It also makes up a good part of your bones and teeth, and benefits bone strength by regulating your levels of calcium and other bone-friendly nutrients such as potassium and vitamin D. Grains supply much of the magnesium in people's diets (and even then, many Americans don't get enough), so on the grain-free Paleo diet, alternate magnesium sources such as macadamia nuts become even more important.

MACADAMIA NUT OIL

Because most Paleo followers avoid industrial seed oils (see page 174), we rely heavily on healthier fats such as coconut oil, ghee (clarified butter), and olive oil. But macadamia nut oil might just convince you to expand your Paleo repertoire. Cold-pressed, organic macadamia nut oil boasts an incredibly delicious, rich flavor that makes it a great alternative to olive oil in cooking, in Paleo baking, in salad dressings, drizzled over vegetables, or even in mayonnaise (see recipe, page 178). And because most of its fats are monounsaturated and quite stable, macadamia nut oil has a high smoke point (around 410°F [210°C], compared to 375°F [190°C] for extra-virgin olive oil, for example), which makes it a super option for high-heat cooking.

GETTING THE MOST OUT OF YOUR MACADAMIA NUTS

Because of macadamia nuts' exceptionally high fat content, proper storage is a must to keep them from going rancid. And that means keeping them cold. You can store unopened containers of macadamia nuts in the refrigerator for up to six months, or in the freezer for up to a year. But once you've opened the package, either freeze them immediately or keep them in the refrigerator and use them within two months. Fresh macadamia nuts should be a creamy white color—if they start to darken, that's a clue they're beginning to go rancid.

HOMEMADE MAYONNAISE

Making homemade Paleo mayonnaise is easy and requires only a few ingredients, but it might take a little patience. Take your time with adding the oil to the egg mixture. If you do, your end result will be a light, silky, flavorful, and healthy mayo you can use in salads or on top of grilled meat.

1 egg, at room temperature

1½ tablespoons (23 ml) freshly squeezed lemon juice

½ teaspoon ground mustard powder

1 cup (235 ml) unrefined macadamia nut oil

½ teaspoon sea salt

¼ teaspoon freshly ground black pepper

In blender or food processor, blend the egg, lemon juice, and ground mustard powder. Slowly add the oil, 1 tablespoon (15 ml) at a time, continuing to process. When all the oil has emulsified and you have a creamy mayonnaise, add the salt and pepper to taste.

MAKES 1 CUP (225 G)

TIP:

Look at the expiration date on your eggs. Add about a week and write that date on the lid of your mayonnaise container so you know when to toss it.

OLIVE OIL

Olive oil is a truly ancient food. Olives have been cultivated in the Mediterranean region's ideal climate (a large reason for its continuing popularity in that region) for at least 6,000 years and this delicious, fruity oil has become a favorite worldwide. Although today it's considered a staple of the Mediterranean diet, cold-pressed extra-virgin olive oil (see the section on shopping for olive oil) is an excellent choice for Paleo followers as well—it is mostly monounsaturated fat, and it doesn't have any of the drawbacks of corn, soybean, or industrial seed oils. Olive oil works best in Paleo recipes that don't involve high-heat cooking (it has a smoke point of 375°F [190°C], and high temperatures can affect its flavor), but it's an outstanding choice for salad dressings or drizzled over already cooked foods.

A HEART-HEALTHY CHOICE

Extra-virgin olive oil, or EVOO, does contain a fair amount of linoleic acid, an inflammation-triggering omega-6 fat. However, it's also rich in a monounsaturated fat called oleic acid that helps lower cholesterol and blood pressure and provides other cardiovascular benefits. It contains a wealth of polyphenols (antioxidant plant compounds) that help achieve the Paleo goal of fighting inflammation, including C-reactive protein, an inflammatory marker that indicates heart disease risk. What's more, it doesn't take much to reap olive oil's inflammation-fighting benefits. A 2012 Spanish study that looked at the diets of 40,622 people found that those who consumed about 2 tablespoons (30 ml) of olive oil per day were 44 percent less likely to die of heart disease than people who didn't use olive oil. The researchers noted that

for every 10 grams of olive oil people consumed (that's 2 teaspoons), they were 7 percent less likely to die of any cause and 13 percent less likely to die of heart disease.

Oxidative stress also harms your cardiovascular system, and those powerful polyphenols prove beneficial here, too—research indicates that diets rich in antioxidant polyphenols appear to lower the risk of cardiovascular disease. Free radicals can cause oxygen damage to fat (especially LDL cholesterol, which is one reason why it's often referred to as "bad" cholesterol), in a process called lipid peroxidation. They can also damage the cells that line your blood vessels, making it easier for that oxidized cholesterol to stick to your artery walls and form plaques that block blood flow. But polyphenols directly protect your blood vessels against those effects, notes a 2010 study in the journal *Medical Science Monitor*.

CANCER FIGHTER

The dangerous combination of excessive oxidative stress and low-grade chronic inflammation is enough to initiate certain types of cancer. But the antioxidant, anti-inflammatory polyphenols in olive oil work to reduce your risk. One polyphenol in particular, hydroxytyrosol, stops the normal cell cycle and triggers apoptosis, or programmed cell death, in cancer cells. These two effects keep cancer cells from reproducing unchecked in your body. Another polyphenol, oleocanthal, slowed the spread, migration, and invasion of breast and prostate cancer cells, according to a 2011 laboratory study published in *Planta Medica*. And here again, as little as 1 to 2 tablespoons (15 to 30 ml) of olive oil per day seems to be enough to lower your risk of certain types of cancer, including cancers of the breast, respiratory tract, upper digestive tract, and, to a lesser extent, lower digestive tract (colorectal).

NAVIGATING THE OLIVE OIL AISLE

Shopping for olive oil can be pretty confusing—not only are there different grades available, ranging from extra-virgin to virgin to light, but there's also the complication that some producers dilute their olive oil with cheaper vegetable oils and deodorized olive oils. So what should you look for? I recommend purchasing extra-virgin olive oil, which comes from the first pressing of the olives. It's unrefined and has the best flavor. You should also look for cold-pressed varieties, which ensures that minimal heat was used during processing. Next, scan the label carefully for a logo of an organization that abides by strict quality standards, such as the California Olive Oil Council (COOC) or the International Olive Oil Council (IOOC). You might also see the French AOC, the Italian DOP or DPO, or the Spanish DO, all of which are equally good indications of quality.

OLIVE OIL FOR BONE HEALTH?

Surprisingly, early research in animals indicates that olive oil might help preserve your bones, particularly in postmenopausal women. That's especially good news for those of us living a dairy-free Paleo lifestyle. In the study, researchers removed the ovaries of female rats to induce menopause, then looked at several markers of bone health. The rats that had diets supplemented with olive oil had noticeably less bone deterioration than those who weren't given olive oil. More research is needed to determine whether the effects translate to humans, but it looks like bone health might be one more in a long list of reasons to incorporate this delicious oil into your diet.

Exposure to light and heat can cause olive oil to oxidize and turn rancid, so also look for bottles or packages that are darkly tinted or opaque and that are displayed away from direct or indirect heat sources. And once you get your olive oil home, make sure that you store it away from light and heat as well.

ROSEMARY- AND THYME-INFUSED OLIVE OIL

The abundance of fresh herbs available throughout spring makes it the perfect time to make your own herb-infused oils. I especially like to use woody herbs (such as rosemary) which, as a bonus, are rich in powerful antioxidants.

4 sprigs fresh rosemary

4 sprigs fresh thyme

4 cups (940 ml) extra-virgin olive oil

4 (8-ounce, or 235 ml) glass bottles

Dip the rosemary and thyme in boiling water, and then pat dry.

Add 1 cup (235 ml) of olive oil to each of the glass bottles, leaving a little room at the top. Add 2 sprigs of rosemary to each of 2 of the bottles, and 2 thyme sprigs to each of the remaining 2 bottles. You can also add peppercorns and even red pepper flakes for a more intense flavor. The bottles make beautiful gifts or party favors.

MAKES FOUR 8-OUNCE (235 ML) BOTTLES

6

PALEO SUPER HERBS AND SPICES

Hunter-gatherer societies ate diets naturally low in sodium—instead of using salt to flavor their foods, they relied on herbs and spices. And of course, they didn't eat the processed foods that are the real culprit behind our sky-high sodium levels today. As a result, the sodium intake of a contemporary Paleo diet is approximately 726 milligrams a day, according to a 2002 study in the *Journal of the American Nutraceutical Association*. That's a far cry from the recommended 2,400 milligrams or the average 3,271 milligrams per day actually consumed in the United States.

But the herbs and spices in this section have health benefits far beyond adding (nearly) sodium-free flavor to your food. They provide an astonishing array of antioxidants and plant compounds so powerful that even the small amount you use in a recipe can benefit your health. Read on to discover some of the best choices to incorporate into your Paleo lifestyle.

GARLIC

Garlic is one of the oldest cultivated plants in the world, prized for both its culinary and medicinal uses. One of the earliest documented examples of plants used to treat disease and maintain health, garlic appears in ancient medical texts from countries as diverse as Egypt, Greece, Rome, China, and India. Modern science confirms garlic's health benefits, and we now know that garlic owes its superfood status to the numerous and potent antioxidants it contains, such as sulfur-containing compounds, polyphenols, selenium, and manganese. These antioxidants fight the unstable free radicals that can damage cell membranes and DNA and may contribute to premature aging, heart disease, cancer, and other health problems. Besides its long history of use as both food and medicine, what elevates garlic from superfood to Paleo superfood is its ability to fight the chronic low-grade inflammation caused by our modern diets (full of processed foods, sugar, and digestive-troubling grains and legumes) and modern sedentary lifestyles.

AMAZING ALLICIN

As with most whole foods, garlic has antioxidant and anti-inflammatory abilities that are probably due to its complex mix of nutrients and phytochemicals rather than to a single agent, but researchers have paid special attention to garlic's sulfur-containing compounds. (They're also responsible for its odor.) One compound in particular, allicin, seems to be a superstar. Allicin is formed as soon as raw garlic is crushed, chewed, or cut. Letting crushed or cut garlic sit at room temperature for fifteen minutes before using will allow the full amount of allicin to form. Cooking inactivates allicin and many of the other medicinal compounds in garlic,

so make sure at least some of the garlic you consume is raw or add it last when cooking. (Eating some fresh parsley or a handful of fennel seeds afterward will help cut down on garlic breath.)

IMMUNE BOOSTER

Garlic supports the immune system by enhancing immune cell function and possibly reducing the length and severity of colds and flus, according to a 2012 study in *Clinical Nutrition*. Among other effects, garlic seems to stimulate the production of natural killer cells, a type of white blood cell that is part of your innate immune system (the body's first line of defense against invaders). And lab studies show that it also directly protects against an incredibly wide range of microbes, from fungi and bacteria to viruses and parasites.

HEART PROTECTOR

Allicin improves heart health in several ways, from keeping your blood vessels relaxed and dilated to controlling cholesterol to preventing potentially deadly clots from forming. It's also one of the many Paleo superfoods that helps keep blood sugar in check. Of course, allicin's antioxidant activity calms heart-harming inflammation as well, and it can stimulate the production of glutathione, an antioxidant your liver makes, according to a 2013 study in *Phytotherapy Research*.

But allicin isn't the only heart helper at work here. The antioxidant minerals selenium and manganese also play a role. Selenium, in conjunction with other antioxidants, may help lower levels of LDL ("bad") cholesterol. And being deficient in selenium appears to make atherosclerosis (hardening of the arteries) worse, contributing to heart failure. Manganese is a component of the powerful antioxidant superoxide dismutase (SOD) that protects the lining of your blood vessels from free radical damage—injury that would encourage the buildup of plaques that can lead to heart attack and stroke.

THE GOODS ON GARLIC

Probably the most important thing to keep in mind when purchasing garlic is to buy a whole bulb, rather than the already minced, diced, or ground garlic in jars. Fresh, raw garlic (organic if you can find it) will have the most health benefits, and a better flavor—jarred garlic can taste bitter. Look for bulbs with cloves that are plump and firm, with the papery skin intact. Soft or spongy garlic, or garlic with green shoots coming out of the tops of the cloves is past its prime. Store your garlic in a cool, dry place with good air circulation. To peel garlic cloves, separate however many you need from the bulb and peel off as much of the papery skin as you can easily. Then, you can either trim the end that was attached to the bulb and smash the clove with the flat of a chef's knife to separate the skin, or place the clove(s) in a bowl with a lid (or covered with another bowl) and shake vigorously until the skin falls off.

When cooking garlic, keep in mind that the more cut surfaces are exposed to air, the stronger the flavor and odor. So whole garlic cloves will have a milder, sweeter flavor, while minced garlic will be pretty potent. Garlic burns easily, which turns it bitter, so keep the heat on medium and just cook it briefly— about 30 seconds. Because heat destroys the allicin responsible for garlic's pungency, the longer you cook it, the mellower it will get.

HOW TO STOP YOUR HANDS FROM SMELLING OF GARLIC

Garlic has a particularly persistent—and pungent!— odor, and once you get it on your hands, it can be tough to get rid of. Methods for deodorizing your hands abound, and some are more successful than others. You can wear gloves when you work with raw garlic, or you can try one of these methods from gardening author Jackie French:

Scrub garlicky hands with salt in cold water and lemon juice, then wash with warm soapy water, or place ½ cup (64 g) of baking soda in a blender with the juice of 2 lemons and a bunch of parsley. Blend thoroughly. Keep in a jar in the fridge and dip your fingers in it after peeling garlic. Wash with cold then warm soapy water.

ROASTED BROCCOLI AND CAULIFLOWER WITH GARLIC AND LEMON

Broccoli, cauliflower, and lemons are all rich in vitamin C, and garlic adds antioxidants for a nutrient-packed side dish perfect for any meal.

1 head broccoli (about 1 pound [454 g]), broken into 1-inch (2.5 cm) florets, stalks peeled and thinly sliced

1 large head cauliflower (about 2 pounds [908 g]), broken into florets

2 tablespoons (28 g) coconut oil, melted

4 cloves garlic, thinly sliced

2 lemons, thinly sliced

2 sprigs fresh rosemary

Coarse salt and ground pepper

Preheat the oven to 400°F (200°C, or gas mark 6). On 2 rimmed baking sheets, toss the broccoli and cauliflower with the coconut oil, garlic, lemons, and rosemary; season with salt and pepper.

Roast until the vegetables are browned and tender, 25 to 30 minutes, rotating the sheets from top to bottom and tossing the vegetables once halfway through. Remove the rosemary sprigs and serve immediately.

MAKES 4 SERVINGS

PARSLEY

Native to the Mediterranean region, parsley was used by the ancient Greeks and Romans as a flavoring and garnish. In the millennia since, parsley continued to feature prominently in the cuisines of Greece, Turkey, the Middle East, and North Africa, but Americans have come to think of it as more of a decorative herb than anything else. Parsley is way more than a garnish, however—this super-powered herb definitely deserves to be called a Paleo superfood. A great alternative to adding salt to your recipes (something our Paleolithic ancestors rarely, if ever, did), parsley gives a fresh, bright flavor to fish, meats, soups, salads, and sauces. Rich in vitamins A, C, and K, parsley also features volatile oils and flavonoids that confer some stellar health benefits.

Although these actions are especially critical given the Paleo diet's lack of calcium-rich dairy products, an active Paleo lifestyle may also increase your need for vitamin K. Strenuous exercise can cause low peak bone mass and rapid bone loss. But in a study of elite female athletes, supplementing with vitamin K increased osteocalcin's ability to bind with calcium to form bone, and researchers noted an improved balance between bone formation and bone loss.

BOOST YOUR BONES

Just 1 tablespoon (4 g) of fresh parsley contains a remarkable 77 percent (61.5 micrograms) of your daily amount of vitamin K. However, some experts point out that the dietary recommendations were set to ensure your body would have enough vitamin K for your blood to coagulate and clot, but that we might actually need more to reap all of its bone benefits. For example, getting enough vitamin K in your diet helps preserve your bone mineral density and reduces your risk of fractures, notes a 2008 study in the journal *Vitamins and Hormones*. That's because vitamin K helps activate a protein called osteocalcin involved in bone formation, and it ensures that osteoblasts (bone-forming cells) can work properly. Parsley also contains small amounts of calcium and potassium to strengthen bones.

VOLATILE OILS

Parsley contains several valuable volatile oils with funny-sounding names such as myristicin, limonene, eugenol, and alpha-thujene. These oils give parsley its characteristic flavor, and they also act as antioxidants and help minimize your risk of cancer. Animal studies suggest that one volatile oil in particular, myristicin, activates a detoxification enzyme called glutathione S-transferase that inhibits tumor formation. Parsley's volatile oils also help neutralize specific kinds of carcinogens, such as the benzopyrenes that are part of smoke from cigarettes and charcoal grills. (More reason to serve a parsley-laden side dish at your next cookout!) Lab studies show that myristicin is antibacterial and anti-inflammatory as well, providing special benefit to your immune system, notes a 2011 study in the journal *Molecules*.

FLAVONOIDS

One of parsley's primary flavonoids, apigenin, also shows antioxidant and anti-carcinogenic effects. Your cells can handle a certain amount of oxidative stress, with mechanisms in place throughout the cell life cycle to protect your DNA against free radical attacks. But when you encounter more free radicals than your body can defuse, they can interfere with the normal cell cycle and turn your cells cancerous. Apigenin is able to help regulate certain checkpoints throughout the cell cycle that ensure the cell, including its DNA, is reproducing properly, according to a 2008 study in *Frontiers of Bioscience*. And parsley's family of flavonoids (especially one called luteolin) helps protect against cell damage that's linked to other diseases as well, including asthma, atherosclerosis, diabetes, glaucoma, and macular degeneration.

PICKING PERFECT PARSLEY

The two most popular types are curly parsley and Italian flat leaf parsley, with the Italian variety being more fragrant and less bitter, with a slightly peppery, grassy flavor. It also holds up better to heat—one reason why curly parsley is more often used as a garnish. Purchase parsley that has vibrant green leaves and stems—pass on bunches that are yellowing or wilting. To store it, wash uncut parsley stems well with cold water, then pat dry gently with paper towels. Loosely roll the bunch in damp paper towels in a resealable plastic bag; they'll keep for up to a week. When you're ready to use it, pick the parsley leaves off the stems (discard the tough stems) and use whole or chop as needed. Add fresh parsley to finished dishes (or at least at the very end of cooking) to preserve its flavor.

PRESERVING PARSLEY

Dried parsley is honestly pretty bland, but if you can't use up all the fresh parsley you've bought, you can freeze it for up to a year. Simply chop your parsley, spoon into an ice cube tray (packing the leaves pretty tightly), and slowly pour water over the herbs to cover. Freeze overnight, transfer the cubes to an airtight container, then pop them back in the freezer to store. You can drop one or two of these parsley cubes into soups or sauces all year long.

SHRIMP, ASPARAGUS, AND TOMATO SALAD WITH PARSLEY-HERB DRESSING

This is a great spring or summertime salad, bright with color and packed with many Paleo superfoods. It makes a tasty light meal on its own, or you can serve it as a side salad to a larger meal.

FOR SALAD:

½ bunch asparagus, chopped

1 cup (150 g) cherry tomatoes, halved

2 teaspoons olive oil, divided

Sea salt and pepper to taste

1 pound (454 g) wild-caught shrimp, peeled and deveined

1 small zucchini, diced

1 clove garlic, minced

1 or 2 scallions, sliced

¼ cup (10 g) fresh basil, chopped

¼ cup (15 g) fresh parsley, chopped

FOR PARSLEY-HERB DRESSING:

⅓ cup (20 g) fresh parsley, tightly packed

⅓ cup (13 g) fresh basil, tightly packed

2 tablespoons (30 ml) apple cider vinegar

1 tablespoon (11 g) gluten-free Dijon mustard

1 teaspoon minced garlic

¼ teaspoon sea salt

¼ cup (60 ml) extra-virgin olive oil

Freshly ground pepper to taste

To make the salad: Preheat the oven to 400°F (200°C, or gas mark 6). Toss the asparagus pieces and halved cherry tomatoes in 1 teaspoon of the olive oil. Sprinkle with a little salt and pepper and toss again to coat. Spread in a single layer on a baking sheet and roast for 5 minutes, or until the asparagus is tender. Place the warm vegetables in a large bowl.

While the vegetables are roasting, toss the shrimp in the remaining 1 teaspoon olive oil. Heat a large skillet over medium-high heat and sauté the shrimp for 2 to 3 minutes, or until opaque in the center. Remove from the heat and place in the bowl with the asparagus mixture.

Add the zucchini, garlic, scallions, basil, parsley, and more salt and pepper to the bowl and toss to combine.

To make the dressing: In the bowl of a food processor, combine the parsley, basil, apple cider vinegar, mustard, garlic, and salt. While the food processor is running, slowly add the olive oil in a small drizzle. You may have to stop the food processor to scrape down the sides of the bowl. Keep processing until the dressing comes together in a liquid consistency. Add freshly ground pepper to taste. Add the dressing to the shrimp salad and toss to combine. Serve immediately or chill and enjoy later.

MAKES 6 TO 8 SERVINGS

CINNAMON

Cinnamon is one of my favorite spices, with its sweet, woody, and warm aroma that's somehow both delicate and intense. It has a long history as both a flavoring agent and a medicine (Chinese medicine has relied on cinnamon for thousands of years, for example). Paleo followers appreciate it today for both its ability to satisfy a sweet tooth without added sugar and its many health benefits, including antimicrobial, antifungal, antiviral, antioxidant, antitumor, blood pressure–lowering, cholesterol and lipid-lowering, and gastro-protective properties. Whew!

Of the numerous species of cinnamon, Ceylon (sometimes called true cinnamon) and cassia (Chinese cinnamon) are the two most popular. And they're surprisingly versatile—Ceylon cinnamon's slightly sweet flavor lends itself well to Paleo baking, and cassia cinnamon works well for adding depth to savory dishes. In fact, you'll find cinnamon in decidedly non-sweet spice blends from around the world, such as Chinese five-spice powder, Indian curries, and Moroccan stews. Sprinkle cinnamon over a baked sweet potato, carrots, or squash to highlight their natural sweetness; add a pinch to your coffee beans before brewing; add a dash to leafy winter greens to curb their bitterness; or try my All-Purpose Spice Rub (see sidebar) the next time you grill.

BLOOD SUGAR BENEFITS

If you've "gone Paleo" in an effort to prevent or reverse diabetes, cinnamon is your new preferred spice. Out of all the medicinal uses for cinnamon, its effect on blood sugar is the most widely studied. Lab and animal studies show that cinnamon might benefit people with metabolic syndrome and type 2 diabetes because it can help improve insulin resistance (it works in a similar way to a popular class of drugs used to treat type 2 diabetes). And studies in people indicate that consuming cinnamon improves fasting blood sugar levels. For example, diabetic patients who consumed 1 gram of cinnamon a day—a definitely doable ½ teaspoon—for forty days reduced their fasting glucose levels by anywhere from 18 to 29 percent in a 2003 study in the journal *Diabetes Care*. (Higher amounts of cinnamon didn't show additional advantage.) And cinnamon seems to have similar benefits for people with prediabetes, according to a 2011 review in the *Journal of Medicinal Food*.

However, human trials have found varying results for some of cinnamon's effects on other symptoms of diabetes, such as cholesterol levels, systolic blood pressure, insulin sensitivity, and blood sugar levels after eating. But because cinnamon seems so promising in these areas—and because diabetes is increasingly becoming a modern epidemic worldwide—researchers are actively conducting more and better studies to determine exactly how cinnamon can help.

ANTIOXIDANT EFFECTS

Cinnamon boasts a good amount of the antioxidant mineral manganese (1 teaspoon contains 22 percent of your recommended daily amount) and several powerful antioxidant polyphenols. These potent compounds make cinnamon an excellent free radical fighter. For instance, compared with several other "dessert spices" and three chemical food preservatives, cinnamon (along with mint) was tops at preventing lipid peroxidation, the free radical damage to fats that's linked to atherosclerosis and several other diseases. Cinnamon also proved the most effective against superoxide radicals, a highly reactive type of free radical.

Cinnamon's antioxidants help calm inflammation, which may pose special benefits for Paleo followers who do intense exercise. Athletes who consumed 3 grams (about 1½ teaspoons) of cinnamon daily for six weeks reported significantly less muscle soreness after exercise than those who took a placebo, according to a 2013 study in the *International Journal of Preventive Medicine*.

BRAIN BOOSTER

Cinnamon may also benefit your brain. Researchers at Wheeling Jesuit University found that smelling cinnamon can improve alertness, memory, and response speed on a test to measure cognitive function. And early evidence suggests that cinnamon could help with Alzheimer's and Parkinson's diseases as well.

STOCK UP ON CINNAMON

Supermarkets tend to carry cassia cinnamon in both stick and powdered form. To find the sweeter Ceylon variety, you'll probably have to visit a spice store or an ethnic market. Stored in tightly sealed glass jars in a cool, dark, and dry place, cinnamon sticks will keep for about a year, and ground cinnamon will last for about six months. The best test for freshness is to smell it—fresh cinnamon should smell sweet.

BONUS RECIPE

True to its name, this all-purpose rub works equally well with all kinds of foods, from meat to poultry, seafood to vegetables.

ALL-PURPOSE SPICE RUB

¼ cup (30 g) chili powder

1 teaspoon ground cinnamon

½ teaspoon ground cumin

½ teaspoon dry mustard

½ teaspoon dried oregano

1 teaspoon sea salt

In a small bowl, combine all of the rub ingredients. Add enough fat/oil of your choice (coconut oil, olive oil, or macadamia nut oil) to make a paste and rub over raw meat, under and over chicken skin, or on seafood, or toss it with cut vegetables. Cook as desired.

MAKES ¾ CUP (78 G)

APPLE CINNAMON "OATMEAL"

Both apples and cinnamon offer significant health benefits, partly due to their high levels of antioxidants. The pairing works great for those cool fall mornings when all you want is something warm to eat. This grain-free version of the traditional oatmeal is sure to keep you fueled until lunch.

4 dates, pitted and mashed

½ cup plus 2 tablespoons (150 ml) coconut milk, divided

½ cup (120 ml) water

1 egg

1 teaspoon vanilla extract

¼ cup (32 g) coconut flour

1 teaspoon ground cinnamon

1 small apple, shredded

¼ cup (20 g) unsweetened shredded coconut

Toasted pecans (optional)

In the bowl of a food processor, place the dates, ½ cup (120 ml) of the coconut milk, water, egg, and vanilla extract and process until smooth and the dates are completely broken up. Add the coconut flour and cinnamon to the bowl of the food processor and pulse to combine with the wet ingredients. Remove the blade from the food processor and stir in the shredded apple and shredded coconut.

Pour the apple mixture into a saucepan and cook over medium heat for 3 to 4 minutes, stirring constantly (don't overcook or the oatmeal will become too dry). Add the remaining 2 tablespoons (30 ml) coconut milk and stir to incorporate.

Divide between 2 bowls and top with the toasted pecans, if using, and a dash or two of ground cinnamon.

MAKES 2 SERVINGS

TIP:

Adding toasted pecans adds a nice crunch to the oatmeal. To toast pecans, preheat the oven to 350°F (180°C, or gas mark 4) and spread out the pecans in a single layer on the baking sheet. Bake for 8 to 10 minutes, or until fragrant and lightly browned.

CAYENNE PEPPER

Cayenne pepper, a member of the *Capsicum* species that originated in Central and South America, can turn up the heat in some of your favorite Paleo dishes. It also enhances flavor—helpful because Paleo cooking uses so little added salt. As you might have guessed, cayenne offers substantial health benefits as well. Native Americans have used cayenne in cooking and medicinally for at least 9,000 years, and traditional Indian Ayurvedic, Chinese, Japanese, and Korean cultures used cayenne to treat stomach problems, poor appetite, and circulatory problems. Today, cayenne is popular in Cajun and Creole cooking, and in the cuisines of Southeast Asia, China, southern Italy, and Mexico. And you can easily incorporate it into other foods—add a dash to your morning eggs, keep a shaker at the table and use cayenne in place of black pepper, or even add a pinch to your Paleo hot cocoa. It may take a while to get used to the heat, so start with small amounts and add more over time.

CAPITALIZE ON CAPSAICIN

A compound called capsaicin is to blame for the burning sensation in your mouth when you eat cayenne pepper—the hotter the pepper, the more capsaicin it contains. But capsaicin does more than spice up your food. As the most active compound in cayenne, capsaicin calms inflammation and lowers levels of a chemical that carries pain messages to the brain, called substance P. It's so effective, in fact, that the majority of studies on capsaicin focus on its topical use to relieve the pain of arthritis, diabetic neuropathy, trigeminal neuralgia, shingles, and cluster headaches.

Capsaicin may also help relieve the discomfort and nausea associated with functional dyspepsia,

according to a 2002 study in the *New England Journal of Medicine*. In the study, people who took 2.5 grams of cayenne pepper powder daily (about 1¼ teaspoons) for two weeks reported an average of 60 percent improvement in their symptoms. The researchers suspect that capsaicin worked by desensitizing specific nerve fibers in the gastric system.

Animal and lab evidence suggests that capsaicin might help prevent cancer as well. Although researchers aren't yet sure exactly how capsaicin works, studies show that it inhibits the activity of carcinogens and induces apoptosis (programmed cell death—an important step in keeping cancerous cells from spreading) in numerous cancer cell lines both in the lab and when transferred into rodents.

SUPERCHARGE YOUR IMMUNE SYSTEM

Gram for gram, cayenne contains more vitamin C than an orange. Your body needs vitamin C to help your immune system function properly, but it's also an especially effective antioxidant because it can regenerate other antioxidants in the body, such as the flavonoids and carotenoids (pigments that give red, yellow, and orange plants their color) that cayenne also contains. These powerful plant compounds help calm inflammation —a primary characteristic of Paleo superfoods—and fight free radicals that impair your immunity. Your body converts some of cayenne's carotenoids into vitamin A, making cayenne an excellent source of this vitamin as well, with 15 percent of your daily recommended amount in just a teaspoon. Sometimes called the anti-infection vitamin, vitamin A helps protect your epithelial cells (cells that line many of your organs), especially the mucous membranes that form a barrier to infectious microorganisms. Low levels of vitamin A can also reduce your numbers of lymphocytes, white blood cells that defend against infection.

Should you end up getting a cold anyway, cayenne can help clear congestion. You know how its spicy heat makes your nose run when you eat it? Those same secretions help break up congestion in your nose and lungs. The next time you get a cold, add some cayenne pepper to your food, or put a pinch in a cup of hot tea—the steam will help, too.

SHOPPING FOR AND STORING CAYENNE

You can find cayenne pepper in just about any supermarket, but if you're a fan of this fiery spice, explore the spice stores or ethnic markets near you. In addition to having fresher spices, they might also have varieties with slightly different flavor profiles, spice blends, or unique suggestions for using cayenne. Purchase organic cayenne to ensure that it hasn't been irradiated (among other potential adverse effects, irradiation kills off the bacteria that produce the smells that warn you when food is no longer fresh). Keep your cayenne in a tightly sealed glass jar, away from direct sunlight.

A NOTE ON NIGHTSHADES

Cayenne pepper can make an excellent addition to your Paleo lifestyle, but keep in mind it is in the nightshade family and may not be for everyone. Nightshades contain compounds called alkaloids that essentially act as natural pesticides. And while some people tolerate them just fine, others are much more sensitive and find that alkaloid-containing foods trigger symptoms such as stomach discomfort and digestive trouble, joint pain, and muscle tremors.

SPICY MUSTARD BBQ SAUCE

This delicious homemade Paleo BBQ sauce skips all the sugar from traditional sauces but delivers a ton of flavor and spice, thanks to the cayenne (which is also a good source of vitamins A, B_6, C, E, and K). The sauce makes a great addition to pulled pork or grilled chicken, too.

½ tablespoon bacon grease (or coconut oil)

3 cloves garlic, minced

¼ cup (40 g) minced sweet yellow onion

⅓ cup (55 g) Dijon mustard

1 teaspoon apple cider vinegar

1 teaspoon coconut aminos*

1 teaspoon paprika

¼ teaspoon cayenne pepper

¼ teaspoon sea salt

Juice of 1 lemon

1⅓ cups (315 ml) low-sodium chicken broth

1 jar or can (7 ounces, or 196 g) tomato paste

*See Resources, page 214.

In a saucepan, heat the bacon grease over medium heat. Add the garlic and onion and sauté until the onion is soft and translucent. Add the mustard, apple cider vinegar, coconut aminos, paprika, cayenne pepper, and salt, and continue to sauté for about 30 seconds. Add the lemon juice, chicken broth, and tomato paste, and whisk together until smooth. Bring to a light boil, reduce to a simmer, and slightly cover with a lid. Simmer for 30 to 45 minutes, until the desired consistency, and let cool.

The sauce can be stored in an airtight container in the refrigerator for up to 1 week.

MAKES 2 CUPS (520 G)

BASIL

Originating in the tropical regions of Asia and Africa, basil still thrives in hot and sunny climates, which may be why we view it as a quintessential summer herb. Basil ranks high in popularity for its bright, fresh flavor—it's a natural with tomatoes, and it's great in salads, sauces, and pesto (see page 52)—but its nutrients and essential oils make it a standout for health as well. From its well-documented medicinal properties to its traditional uses, basil more than earns its spot as a Paleo superfood.

ANTI-INFLAMMATORY

If there's one thing the Paleo diet is good at, it's calming harmful inflammation, thanks to its emphasis on healthy fats, antioxidants, and beneficial plant compounds. And basil fits right in—it contains a number of compounds that fight inflammation, including two essential oil components called eugenol and rosmarinic acid. Besides defending your body against oxidative damage, these two compounds decrease the activity of the cyclooxygenase-1 and -2 (COX-1 and -2) enzymes that spur production of inflammatory cells and lead to much of the pain associated with arthritis and other inflammation-related conditions. In high enough concentrations, eugenol and rosmarinic acid have pain-relieving potential comparable to that of ibuprofen, naproxen, and aspirin, according to a 2000 study in the journal *Phytomedicine*.

What's more, basil contains anti-inflammatory, heart-healthy omega-3 fatty acids. And even though the overall amount is small (about 17 milligrams in 2 tablespoons [5 g] of chopped basil), it's more than four times as much as the pro-inflammatory omega-6 fatty acids that basil supplies. In your overall dietary picture, that bit of basil will help you get closer to the Paleo ideal ratio of 2:1 (or even 1:1) of omega-6s to omega-3s.

ANTIMICROBIAL

Basil's essential oil components not only fight free radicals, but they also protect against viruses, fungi, and harmful bacteria. In fact, basil oil proves so effective against these microbes—including nasty bugs such as *Salmonella, E. coli, Listeria*, and *Staphylococcus*—that food manufacturers are investigating using it to protect packaged foods such as fresh meats, fish, and ready-to-eat vegetables against foodborne pathogens and bacteria that cause spoilage. That also means basil makes an excellent addition to uncooked foods such as salads, either as whole leaves mixed in with your other greens or in salad dressings. Washing your fruits and vegetables with a solution containing basil oil will help eliminate microbes as well, according to a 2004 study in the *International Journal of Food Microbiology*.

BONE BUILDING

If you're concerned that the dairy-free Paleo diet will put you at increased risk for osteoporosis, make basil a regular part of your meals. Just 2 tablespoons (5 g) of chopped basil provides more than a quarter of your daily recommended amount of bone-strengthening vitamin K, plus smaller amounts of calcium, magnesium, and potassium critical for bone health.

BEST OF THE BASIL

Fresh, organic basil is far superior to dried, and although you can find it in supermarkets year-round, it's at its best during hot, sunny months. You can also grow your own in the garden or extend its season by planting it indoors in a bright, warm spot. Depending on the variety (there are some sixty different kinds, with sweet basil being the most popular), fresh basil may have accents of clove, citrus, licorice, or cinnamon. When purchasing basil, give it a sniff to verify that those aromas will blend with any other ingredients you're using. Look for deep green leaves without any dark spots or yellowing (white flowers are okay). Some varieties may have tinges of red or purple on the leaves.

Harvest only as much as you need, or store your basil at room temperature—not in the refrigerator, or it will turn black and slimy. I keep my bunches of basil in short, stout vases of water away from direct sunlight. Don't worry if the leaves droop at first—they'll perk up after about twelve hours. If you change the water every other day and harvest as needed (just pinch the stem right above a pair of leaves), the basil should last for a week or more. It might even start to root, at which point you can plant it in a pot or in the garden.

To preserve its flavor and bright green color, add basil near the end of cooking or as a garnish after you've removed your food from the heat.

FREEZE!

If you have more fresh basil than you can use, your best bet is to freeze it rather than dry it. Simply chop the leaves and loosely pack them into an ice cube tray. Cover with oil and place in the freezer. Once frozen, transfer the cubes to a resealable plastic bag or other airtight container for long-term storage. Alternatively, you can process the leaves with olive oil in a food processer and freeze in cubes that way. You can add frozen basil to soups, sauces, or pesto—or you can make fresh basil directly into pesto (minus the garlic) and freeze that, adding fresh garlic when you thaw it.

ARCTIC CHAR WITH SAUTÉED TOMATOES AND BASIL

Nothing quite surpasses tomatoes adorned with fresh basil leaves and garlic. Arctic char is a wonderful fish that looks like salmon but tastes like trout. It supplies protein to rev your metabolism, along with a plentiful dose of omega-3 fats, which benefit your body from head to toe.

¼ cup (60 ml) extra-virgin olive oil

Juice of 1 lemon

2 cloves garlic, minced, divided

½ teaspoon sea salt, divided

½ teaspoon freshly ground black pepper, divided

4 pieces (4 to 6 ounces, or 112 to 168 g) arctic char fillets

1 pint (300 g) cherry tomatoes, halved

¼ cup (10 g) fresh basil, chopped

½ tablespoon olive oil or coconut oil, melted

In a small bowl, whisk together the extra-virgin olive oil, lemon juice, 1 of the minced garlic cloves, ¼ teaspoon of the sea salt, and ¼ teaspoon of the pepper. Placed the washed fish fillets in a resealable plastic bag and add the oil and lemon mixture. Let marinate for 15 to 20 minutes.

Heat an indoor grill pan over medium-high heat. Place the arctic char skin side up onto the heated grill pan, discarding the marinade. Grill for 3 to 4 minutes and carefully flip to cook on the other side for another 3 to 4 minutes, until the fish is just cooked through. You can carefully remove the skin from the fish with a spatula before serving.

While the fish is cooking, prepare the tomato-basil mixture. In a small bowl, toss together the cherry tomatoes, basil, remaining 1 minced garlic clove, remaining ¼ teaspoon sea salt, remaining ¼ teaspoon pepper, and olive oil or coconut oil. Heat a skillet over medium-high heat and sauté the tomato-basil mixture, stirring frequently, for 2 to 3 minutes, or until the tomatoes are just softened and the skins blister.

Divide the fish among 4 plates and top with the tomato-basil mixture.

MAKES 4 SERVINGS

TIP:

This is great served on a bed of spinach or julienned zucchini that has been sautéed for 2 to 3 minutes, or just till softened. Another great option is to serve it over the Spring Veggie Paleo Pasta (page 109).

TURMERIC

Turmeric, a relative of ginger, has a long history of use as both food and medicine. A compound called curcumin provides most of turmeric's health benefits, as well as its characteristic bright yellow color (it gives yellow mustard its hue). In cooking, you'll typically find turmeric in curries and other Indian and Middle Eastern dishes, but its pleasantly bitter flavor adds depth to foods from all culinary traditions, such as soups, sauces, marinades, and egg dishes, so you can go easy on the salt—like our Paleolithic ancestors did.

Ayurveda (the Indian system of medicine) has used turmeric as a healing agent for centuries, and Paleo followers prize turmeric for its anti-inflammatory action, as well. Research on curcumin has exploded in the past decade as scientists investigate its potential to help all kinds of inflammation-related conditions, from arthritis, cardiovascular disease, and cancer, to type 2 diabetes and neurodegenerative diseases, according to a 2013 review in the journal *BioFactors*.

Researchers have noted that curcumin isn't very bioavailable, but consuming turmeric along with black pepper significantly increases your body's ability to use curcumin (by up to 2,000 percent!), and healthy fats may enhance absorption as well. Another tip: cooking turmeric in water or another liquid for ten minutes improves curcumin's bioavailability twelvefold, so add turmeric to soups, sauces, and other dishes at the beginning of cooking to give it time to simmer.

KEEP YOUR BRAIN HEALTHY

Lab and animal studies indicate that curcumin protects the brain in at least ten different ways, including by acting as an antioxidant and combating inflammation. It might also reverse some of the memory and learning problems brought on by chronic stress, according to a 2009 study in the journal *Neuropharmacology*. And a 2008 review of lab and animal studies on the role of curcumin in Alzheimer's found that the spice might improve memory by delaying the breakdown of neurons, decreasing plaque formation, removing toxic metals such cadmium and lead, calming inflammation, and fighting free radicals. Clinical trials are underway to see whether curcumin works the same way in humans, with a handful of very small studies showing promise. Researchers are also encouraged by the fact that the prevalence of Alzheimer's disease in India (where turmeric is a popular spice as a principal ingredient in curry powder) is about 4.4 times lower than that in Western countries, where people don't consume turmeric as often.

PUT A STOP TO PAIN

Traditionally used in Ayurvedic medicine to calm inflammation and relieve pain in the skin and muscles, turmeric is an especially valuable spice for Paleo followers who suffer from muscle soreness after intense exercise. Curcumin attacks inflammation on several fronts, from preventing the spread of inflammatory cells to inhibiting enzymes that promote inflammation.

For example, curcumin appears to bind directly with the pro-inflammatory enzyme cyclooxygenase-2 (COX-2), limiting its ability to trigger the pain and stiffness associated with arthritis. And in one small study in the journal *Surgical Endoscopy*, researchers gave either curcumin capsules or a placebo to patients recovering from surgery. Patients who took the curcumin needed fewer prescription pain medications and rated themselves less fatigued during their recovery.

KEEP CANCER AT BAY

Normal, healthy cells turn over an average of every 100 days, but cancerous cells evade the signals that tell them it's time to die, so they continue to replicate and spread unchecked. Curcumin is able to target the genes that regulate cell proliferation and apoptosis (programmed cell death) to not only prevent cells from becoming cancerous but also to selectively target tumor cells to keep them from spreading, according to a 2009 study in the *AAPS Journal*. That's especially good news because traditional cancer treatments such as chemotherapy target all of your cells—not just the cancerous ones—which accounts for the sometimes brutal side effects. And thanks to the many different ways in which it works, curcumin appears to protect against several kinds of cancer, including leukemia and lymphoma, gastrointestinal cancers, genitourinary cancers, breast cancer, ovarian cancer, head and neck squamous cell carcinoma, lung cancer, melanoma, neurological cancers, and sarcoma, notes a 2008 study in the journal *Cancer Letters*.

TRYING OUT TURMERIC

You can find ground turmeric in any supermarket, but local spice stores or ethnic markets might carry other varieties that have slightly different colors and flavor profiles, or even the fresh rhizome. Buying organic turmeric ensures that it hasn't been irradiated (irradiation, among other potential ill effects, can make it difficult to tell the freshness of the spice). Store ground turmeric in an airtight container in a cool, dark, and dry place. Keep the fresh rhizome in the refrigerator.

BONUS RECIPES

These simple recipes make it easy to add turmeric to your Paleo diet, and the black pepper and healthy fats in the mayonnaise boost your body's ability to use curcumin.

HOMEMADE CURRY POWDER

4 teaspoons coriander seeds

2 teaspoons turmeric

1 teaspoon cumin seeds

2 teaspoons chili powder

½ teaspoon cardamom, exterior pods removed

¼ teaspoon ground cloves

Place all the spices in a mortar and pestle or spice grinder and grind into a fine powder. Store in an airtight container in a cool, dry place.

MAKES 1½ ounces (45 g)

CURRIED MAYONNAISE MARINADE

1 medium onion, finely chopped

1 cup (225 g) mayonnaise (page 178)

¼ cup (60 ml) fresh lemon juice

1 tablespoon (6 g) curry powder (above, or your favorite brand)

½ teaspoon sea salt

¼ teaspoon freshly ground black pepper

Combine all the ingredients in a shallow bowl or baking dish. You can use it to marinate meat or poultry, covered in the refrigerator, for at least 30 minutes and up to overnight. You can also use it as a seafood marinade, but only marinate for 15 to 20 minutes. Cook on a preheated grill to your desired doneness.

MAKES 1½ CUPS (340 G)

TURMERIC-ROASTED CAULIFLOWER WITH CHERRY TOMATOES

This aromatic dish is warming, full of flavor, and nutritious, and makes a wonderful side dish to the protein of your choice. It is also very easy to prepare and looks beautiful brought to the table. The healthy fats and black pepper in this recipe boost your body's ability to use curcumin, the compound in turmeric responsible for most of its health benefits.

1 medium to large head cauliflower, outer leaves removed and cut into florets

1 pint (300 g) cherry tomatoes, washed and halved

2 cloves garlic, minced

2 bay leaves

2 tablespoons (28 g) ghee, melted (or fat/oil of choice)

1 tablespoon (15 ml) lemon juice

1 tablespoon (6 g) ground turmeric

½ teaspoon celery seed

½ teaspoon ground sweet paprika

¼ teaspoon ground cumin

⅛ teaspoon ground cinnamon

Sea salt and pepper to taste

¼ cup (15 g) fresh flat-leaf parsley, chopped, plus more for garnish

Preheat the oven to 350°F (180°C, or gas mark 4). Line a baking sheet with parchment paper.

In a large mixing bowl, place the cauliflower, tomatoes, garlic, and bay leaves.

In a small bowl, mix together the ghee, lemon juice, turmeric, celery seed, sweet paprika, cumin, cinnamon, sea salt, and pepper and pour over the vegetables. Toss well to make sure the vegetables are evenly coated. Spread the mixture on the prepared baking sheet and roast for 30 to 35 minutes, or until the cauliflower florets are golden.

Remove from the oven and discard the bay leaves. Then sprinkle with parsley and serve.

MAKES 6 SERVINGS

MUSTARD SEED

While most of us think of mustard as merely a condiment for burgers and hot dogs, the tiny little mustard seed is actually a member of the seriously impressive *Brassica* family, along with nutritional superstars broccoli, cabbage, and kale. (That might explain why mustard pairs so well with those vegetables!) Besides being a delicious accompaniment to meats and cheeses, mustard is a popular addition to soups, sauces, glazes, marinades, and dressings in cuisines worldwide.

One of the first domesticated crops, mustard has been grown in Asia, North Africa, and Europe for thousands of years. Ancient Greeks and Romans enjoyed it as both a powder and a paste—most likely the precursor to the mustard we enjoy today. Both whole mustard seeds and the ground powder offer similar health benefits. In addition to providing a respectable amount of fiber and iron, mustard seeds are a very good source of phosphorus, calcium, and magnesium important for bones and teeth (especially in the absence of dairy) and proper muscle function to support an active Paleo lifestyle. And they contain several substances that you won't find on the nutrition facts label, but that helps make mustard one of the healthiest spices around.

CANCER PREVENTER

Like other *Brassica*, or cruciferous, vegetables, mustard seeds are rich in sulfur-containing compounds called glucosinolates. Mustard seed contains a glucosinolate called sinigrin, which your body breaks down into a substance called allyl isothiocyanate. As a group, the isothiocyanates (besides giving mustard its pungency) show a powerful ability to prevent chemically induced cancers by neutralizing carcinogens. They also help stop the spread of cancer cells

by triggering apoptosis, or programmed cell death (a natural regulatory mechanism that cancer cells are especially good at escaping). For example, in an animal model, mustard seed powder inhibited bladder cancer growth by 34.5 percent by causing apoptosis and interrupting the cell growth cycle, according to a 2010 study in the journal *Carcinogenesis*. Isothiocyanates have also proven effective against certain pulmonary and forestomach cancers in mice, esophageal cancer in rats, and lung cancer in animals exposed to carcinogens in tobacco smoke, according to a 2003 study in *Carcinogenesis*. That same study also found that allyl isothiocyanate, in particular, helped stop the proliferation of human prostate cancer cells in the lab. More research is needed to see whether mustard works the same way in humans.

INFLAMMATION FIGHTER

Chronic, low-grade inflammation contributes to a wide range of modern diseases, including obesity, cardiovascular disease, type 2 diabetes, and some types of cancer. Like many of its fellow Paleo superfoods, mustard works to quell that inflammation. Mustard seeds supply antioxidants, such as the minerals manganese and selenium, that calm inflammation from free radical attacks. And just 1 teaspoon of these diminutive seeds packs 87 milligrams of anti-inflammatory omega-3 fatty acids (not only that, but mustard seeds contain omega-6 and omega-3 fats in a nearly perfect 1:1 ratio, which is the ideal balance that the Paleo diet tries to maintain).

MAKING THE MOST OF MUSTARD

Out of the forty-some varieties of mustard, three are most commonly used: white mustard seeds, which are actually yellow in color and have the mildest flavor; the slightly stronger-flavored brown mustard seeds used to make Dijon mustard; and the pungent black mustard seeds often used in Indian cooking. You'll likely only find white mustard seeds and ground mustard powder made from white mustard seeds at the supermarket. Explore local spice shops or ethnic markets to find brown or black mustard seeds and their powders. Keep mustard seeds and powder in a tightly sealed container in a cool, dark, and dry place. Store prepared mustard in the refrigerator.

Whether you choose popular yellow mustard, tangy Dijon, or fiery English mustard, when purchasing prepared varieties, you'll need to read food labels very closely (a good practice for all Paleo devotees). Packaged condiments often contain subpar ingredients such as sugar, preservatives, and unhealthy oils—not to mention loads of salt. For example, mustard frequently features brown sugar. To make things easier, I try to make my own whenever I can, using the recipe in the sidebar.

BONUS RECIPE

This is a very basic mustard recipe that you can prepare easily before a big cookout. It only takes 1 part water to 1 part mustard powder, and you'll get a nice mustard for gracing those grass-fed burgers. You can play around with the seasonings too, and use different herbs and spices to create different versions. Vinegars or lemon juice will also add a pleasant tanginess, which I happen to enjoy. Adding cold water to mustard powder creates a chemical reaction that releases mustard's potency, so if you'd like yours a little milder, use hot water or add vinegar or another acid to temper the reaction.

SIMPLE MUSTARD

½ cup (72 g) mustard powder

½ cup (120 ml) filtered water

Sea salt and black pepper to taste

Combine the mustard powder, water, and salt and pepper in a bowl and mix well. Optionally, add a bit of chopped parsley, lemon zest, and/or 1 to 2 tablespoons (15 to 30 ml) of your favorite vinegar (such as apple cider vinegar). Let the mustard stand for about 15 minutes before serving.

MAKES ¾ CUP (210 G)

MUSTARD MAPLE HALIBUT WITH SPINACH

This sweet and savory dish is nutrient-packed and comes together in no time, making it perfect for a weekday night. Cooking the spinach briefly preserves its vitamins and enhances the bioavailability of its antioxidants (such as lutein and beta-carotene), while neutralizing some of the nutrient-blocking oxalic acid it contains.

I tablespoon (14 g) coconut oil, divided

3 tablespoons (33 g) brown mustard seeds

2 tablespoons (22 g) Dijon mustard

1 tablespoon (15 ml) maple syrup

2 teaspoons balsamic vinegar

¼ teaspoon sea salt

¼ teaspoon freshly ground black pepper

4 halibut fillets (5 ounces, or 140 g, each)

1 clove garlic, minced

12 cups (360 g) baby spinach

Preheat the oven to 400°F (200°C, or gas mark 6).

In a small nonstick skillet, heat 1 teaspoon (5 g) of the coconut oil over medium-low heat. Add the mustard seeds and stir to coat. Cover and cook until the seeds begin to pop, about 5 minutes. Turn off the heat and let sit, covered, until the popping stops, about 2 minutes. Stir in the Dijon mustard, maple syrup, balsamic vinegar, salt, and pepper; set aside.

Heat 1 teaspoon (5 g) of the coconut oil in an oven-safe nonstick skillet over medium-high heat. Sear the halibut for 1 minute on each side. Remove from the heat and spoon the mustard mixture over the top of the fish. Transfer to the oven and bake until cooked through, about 8 to 10 minutes depending on the thickness. Remove from the oven and loosely tent with foil to keep warm.

Heat a large nonstick skillet over medium-high heat and add the remaining 1 teaspoon (4 g) coconut oil. Add the garlic and sauté, stirring occasionally, for 1 minute. Add the spinach and cook until just wilted, about 2 minutes. Season with salt and pepper. Divide the spinach among 4 serving plates and top with a fillet of fish.

MAKES 4 SERVINGS

TIP:
You can substitute the halibut for cod or another white fish.

RESOURCES

You can obtain many of the ingredients in this book from your local health food store, but you may need other resources from time to time. Listed here are some of my favorite places to find ingredients that are Paleo-friendly. Keep in mind that when you purchase produce from your local farmers' market, most of the suppliers have been required to submit safety records that are in compliance with local, state, and federal regulations—particularly when it comes to meat and dairy. If you buy directly from the farm, you'll have to do that research yourself to ensure that your purchases are from a safe and reliable source.

MEAT AND SEAFOOD

U.S. Wellness Meats—www.grasslandbeef.com

Eat Wild—www.eatwild.com

Proffitt Farms— www.proffittfarms.com

Wild Idea Buffalo—www.wildideabuffalo.com

Vital Choice—www.vitalchoice.com/shop/pc/home.asp

LOCAL PRODUCE

Local Harvest—www.localharvest.org

FATS AND OILS

Coconut Oil—Wilderness Family Naturals (www.wildernessfamilynaturals.com) and Tropical Traditions (www.tropicaltraditions.com)

Ghee—Pure Indian Foods 100% Organic Grass-Fed Ghee (www.purindianfoods.com) and Purity Farms Organic Ghee (www.purityfarms.com)

Macadamia Nut Oil—www.vitalchoice.com

Extra-Virgin Olive Oil—www.mcevoyranch.com

GRAIN-FREE FLOURS

Coconut Flour—Coconut Secret Raw Organic Coconut Flour (www.coconutsecret.com)

Almond Flour and Almond Meal—Honeyville Grain Blanched Almond Flour and Almond Meal (www.honeyvillegrain.com)

SWEETENERS

Maple Syrup—Shady Maple Farms Organic Maple Syrup (www.abesmarket.com)

Honey—Raw Honey (www.reallyrawhoney.com)

OTHER ESSENTIALS

Coconut Milk—Native Forest Organic Coconut Milk (www.edwardandsons.com)

Cacao Powder—www.wildernessfamilynaturals.com and www.rapunzel.com

Coconut Aminos—Coconut Secret Aminos (www.coconutsecret.com)

Organic Nuts—www.nuts.com and Wilderness Family Naturals (www.wildernessfamilynaturals.com)

Organic Shredded Coconut—Let's Do Organic Coconut (www.edwardandsons.com)

Organic Spices—www.organicspices.com and www.simplyorganic.com

Robb Wolf—www.robbwolf.com

Foodee—www.thefoodee.com

Chris Kresser—www.chriskresser.com

Mark's Daily Apple—www.marksdailyapple.com

The Paleo Mom—www.thepaleomom.com

FINDING US

HEATHER:

MultiplyDelicious.com

My first Paleo cookbook: *Paleo Sweets and Treats* (Fair Winds Press, 2013)

Facebook, Pinterest, and Instagram: Multiply Delicious

Twitter: @Multiplydelicio

JULIA:

www.juliamaranan.com

My first book: *The 100 Best Ways to Stop Aging and Stay Young* (Fair Winds Press, 2011)

Facebook: Julia Maranan, author

Twitter: @juliamaranan

OTHER PALEO RESOURCES

Want to learn more about the Paleo lifestyle? These are some of my favorite websites.

PaleOMG—www.paleomg.com

Against All Grain—www.againstallgrain.com

The Urban Poser—www.urbanposer.blogspot.com

Health Bent—www.health-bent.com

Nom Nom Paleo—www.nomnompaleo.com

Paleo Parents—www.paleoparents.com

Balanced Bites—www.balancedbites.com

The Food Lovers Primal Palate—www.primal-palate.com

ACKNOWLEDGMENTS

FROM HEATHER:

There are so many people who have helped in the creation of *Powerful Paleo Superfoods*. Without the help and support of these great people, this book wouldn't have been possible.

To my husband, Scott, thank you for your love, encouragement, and continued support, and for being my taste-tester and telling me your honest opinion. You are an extraordinary person, and I'm so lucky I get to share my life with you . . . my best friend.

To my little girls, I can't even begin to tell you how much I love and adore you both. You have been my little helpers throughout this cookbook, from tasting recipes and giving me a thumbs up or down to helping me measure and mix, all while smiling and giggling. You have no idea how much your spirit and excitement keep me going.

To mom, what can I say? Beginning when I was a little girl you taught me your culinary craft. Even though it took me getting married to actually fall in love with cooking, I will forever be grateful for those times spent in the kitchen as a child. Outside the kitchen, your support, love, encouragement, and guidance have shaped me. Thank you for believing in me every step of the way. You will never know how thankful I am for you and all that you are.

To my friends and family, who span across states and have been the biggest supporters and cheerleaders on this cookbook journey. Without this village of support, which I am very grateful for, none of this would have been possible. It is true that we are only as good as the people who surround us and drive us to be the best versions of ourselves.

A huge thanks to Julia Maranan, my partner in crime in creating this book. You have elegantly put together words to convey exactly what I wanted to say. Thank you for your endless hours helping to perfect this book. I would have never been able to make it all happen without your help, so from the bottom of my heart . . . thank you!

Thanks to my editor, Jill Alexander, at Fair Winds Press, for your continued faith in the Paleo movement and in me. It has been a joy working with you. Thank you for believing in me not once, but twice. I will forever be grateful for your help in giving me the opportunity to spread the Paleo word.

Thank you to each and every one of my blog readers and fans. Your stories of success and notes of appreciation keep me going and make what I do on the blog so special. It is a true joy to continue to create new recipes for you to use in your Paleo journey.

FROM JULIA:

Eternal thanks to my husband, Dan, who tirelessly supported me as I tried to balance writing this book with caring for a new baby. Your encouragement means more than I can say.

To Heather, thanks for the chance to work on this book with you. Your energy and passion for Paleo are inspiring, and I've truly enjoyed collaborating with you. I've also very much enjoyed testing your recipes . . .

Thank you also to Jill Alexander at Fair Winds Press for connecting me with Heather. Writing this book has been a fun, thought-provoking journey, and I'm so happy I had the opportunity to work with Heather and with you and the Fair Winds crew again.

ABOUT THE AUTHORS

HEATHER CONNELL, R.H.N.C., is a busy mom to twin daughters and the creator and voice of Multiply Delicious, a blog where she shares her passion for Paleo cooking and baking. She is also the author of *Paleo Sweets and Treats* (Fair Winds Press, 2013). Heather discovered Paleo after suffering health issues of her own. Just by following the Paleo diet, she regained her health and hasn't looked back since. She is now a certified holistic nutritionist and is committed to educating others on how Paleo can help them live a healthier lifestyle. She enjoys using the knowledge she has gained inside and outside the kitchen to help families incorporate the Paleo lifestyle successfully into their lives.

JULIA MARANAN is an award-winning writer with more than a decade of experience writing about nutrition, fitness, and all things health-related. The author of *The 100 Best Ways to Stop Aging and Stay Young* (Fair Winds Press, 2011) and a former editor at *Natural Health* magazine, she has also written hundreds of articles for national publications, including *AARP the Magazine, Family Circle, Fit Pregnancy, Fitness*, Dr. Andrew Weil's *Self Healing* newsletter, *Shape*, and *Whole Living*.

INDEX